If you want to take your sex life to the next l[...] place. Sheila speaks with candor and offers practical steps to deeper intimacy in a way that not many others do. You'll learn not only to appreciate sexual intimacy but also to seriously enjoy it.

DEBRA FILETA, author of *Love in Every Season*, creator of TrueLoveDates.com

When it comes to sex, Sheila knows her stuff. She writes as she speaks: honestly, wisely, and with lots of helpful information for healthy sexual relationships.

NEIL AND SHAROL JOSEPHSON, directors of FamilyLife Canada

Sex is one form of communication. Many couples find it difficult to talk about this intimate form of communication. In *31 Days to Great Sex*, Sheila Wray Gregoire speaks truth to you about your sex life and will help you and your spouse communicate better about it. God has great things in store for you. Let the communication begin!

RON L. DEAL, marriage trainer, licensed marriage and family therapist, and bestselling author of *The Smart Stepfamily* and *Building Love Together in Blended Families*

As a Christian, I feel like there is a whole conversation going on that I haven't been a part of. That is why I'm so grateful for Sheila Wray Gregoire's fact- and grace-based approach to the topic of sex. And bonus? I'm never embarrassed to refer my friends (no matter their faith background) to her teachings because I know she tells the truth without spin. Shelia is a trusted and powerful voice on the side of truth.

KATHI LIPP, bestselling author of *The Husband Project* and *Clutter Free*

Sheila Gregoire's work is already staple reading for many women, but I hope this book expands her reach to men as well. Sex is a wonderful thing, but Christians in particular either seem to be more than a little reluctant to talk about it or they talk about it in obnoxious and unhelpful ways. Gregoire cuts right down the middle by offering practical, applicable advice for a fuller enjoyment of what Ecclesiastes names one of God's good gifts. I think all men should read this book, along with their wives, and thank God for this good gift he's given married folks.

RUSSELL L. MEEK, speaker, writer, and professor

31
DAYS TO
Great
Sex

Love. Friendship. Fun.

SHEILA WRAY GREGOIRE

ZONDERVAN
BOOKS

ZONDERVAN BOOKS

31 Days to Great Sex
Copyright © 2013, 2020 by Sheila Wray Gregoire

Requests for information should be addressed to:
Zondervan, *3900 Sparks Dr. SE, Grand Rapids, Michigan 49546*

Zondervan titles may be purchased in bulk for educational, business, fundraising, or sales promotional use. For information, please email SpecialMarkets@Zondervan.com.

ISBN 978-0-310-35836-7 (audio)

Library of Congress Cataloging-in-Publication Data

Names: Gregoire, Sheila Wray, 1970- author.
Title: 31 days to great sex : love. friendship. fun. / Sheila Wray Gregoire.
Other titles: Thirty-one days to great sex
Description: Grand Rapids, Michigan : Zondervan, [2020] | Includes bibliographical references. | Summary: "This super practical book gives thirty-one days of challenges for you and your spouse to help you talk, flirt, and explore all three levels of sexual intimacy—physical, emotional, and spiritual—so you both can experience the best sex ever"— Provided by publisher.
Identifiers: LCCN 2020000392 (print) | LCCN 2020000393 (ebook) | ISBN 9780310358343 (trade paperback) | ISBN 9780310358350 (ebook)
Subjects: LCSH: Sex—Religious aspects—Christianity. | Sex in marriage—Religious aspects—Christianity. | Intimacy (Psychology—Religious aspects—Christianity. | Married people—Religious life.
Classification: LCC BT708 .G7135 2020 (print) | LCC BT708 (ebook) | DDC 248.8/44—dc23
LC record available at https://lccn.loc.gov/2020000392
LC ebook record available at https://lccn.loc.gov/2020000393

The author is represented by MacGregor Literary, Inc.

Cover design: Curt Diepenhorst
Cover photos: karakedi35 / Elnur / Shutterstock
Interior design: Denise Froehlich
Author photo: Pics & Tweaks Photography, 2019

To my wonderful To Love, Honor, and Vacuum *readers and commenters, for whom this content was first written and whose comments and emails helped shape it*

Contents

Days 20–26: True Oneness in the Bedroom (Spiritual Intimacy)

Days 27–31: Keep the Momentum Going!

ACKNOWLEDGMENTS

This book wouldn't exist if it weren't for my blog, *To Love, Honor, and Vacuum*. And that blog wouldn't still be thriving after twelve years if it weren't for my faithful readers and commenters. I think of so many of you by name, and I appreciate your comments, encouragement, and emails. When you spend your life curled up in a yellow living room armchair with a cup of tea by your side and a computer balanced on your lap, tap-tap-tapping into space, it can be easy to think no one's really listening. The many, many readers who have replied, commented, and thanked me have changed the direction of my blog, the direction of my thinking, and have shaped me in so many ways. I am very grateful.

This book also would not have come to be had it not been for my first sex book, *The Good Girl's Guide to Great Sex*. As that book launched, I envisioned a blog post series about sex, and it was really that series (which turned into this book) that put my blog on the map. And so I would like to thank Chip MacGregor, my wonderful agent, for helping put me and Zondervan together and Sandra VanderZicht, who first took a risk on a relatively unknown (and Canadian!) blogger.

Since then I've had the privilege to work with other amazing, talented people from Zondervan, especially Carolyn McCready, who was so easy to bounce ideas off of as we tried to adapt the blog series to make it an accessible and helpful book. And she put up with all my Canadian spellings too.

To my mom, Elizabeth Wray, who always tiptoes around the house when I'm working so as not to disturb me, even though it's her house too.

And most especially to my *To Love, Honor, and Vacuum* team: my daughter Rebecca, her husband Connor, Tammy, Joanna, and Emily. You guys had to carry a lot while I worked on this, and I love that I can rely on you. Rebecca, we likely have the strangest mother-daughter relationship I know. Not everyone takes it in stride when their mother calls up and says, "I have a post that needs to be up in fifteen minutes on ten ways to get more adventurous in bed, and I only have eight. What are two more?" And then we brainstorm like that's normal. And for us it is.

And Connor, you didn't know what you were getting into when you married into this family, but few people can talk to their mother-in-law like you can! Thank you for relieving me of some of my biggest technical headaches so I could do what I love to do best—write.

Tammy, thanks for keeping me sane and making sure nothing fell through the cracks.

And Katie, thank you for taking walks with me and helping me process when I was stressed. You've always been so good at that.

And last of all, to Keith, whom I love dearly and who could likely come up with thirty-one more ideas to fill this book. But that's all I'm going to say about that.

INTRODUCTION

Who doesn't want great sex?

To feel swept off your feet, to feel one with another person, to feel physical ecstasy—that sounds heavenly!

But not all of us experience those feelings when we make love with our spouses. Some of us don't feel much pleasure. Some of us have really low sex drives. Some of us feel rejected because our spouse doesn't seem to want sex very often.

No matter where you're coming from, I'm glad you've decided to launch into *31 Days to Great Sex*. This book is intended for married couples who want to experience real intimacy and ecstasy in the bedroom. After all, that's what sex is supposed to be. By focusing on each other, developing new habits (and even new skills!), and dealing with baggage, I believe you can experience sex as God intended.

I've been blogging and writing about sex for over a decade, and as I've listened to many couples struggling with their unsatisfying sex lives, I've noticed some commonalities. I've structured this 31-day challenge to tackle all of those—hopefully with a lot of fun and laughter.

How does this 31-day challenge work? Each day has a new topic and a new challenge. Please do the challenges! Putting principles into practice is far more effective than just reading about them.

The month starts with a week of challenges that frame sex in a positive light. I'm hoping you experience some quick victories that propel you along to learn new habits and techniques. Then we'll turn to challenges relating to the three aspects of intimacy in the bedroom: emotional intimacy (or laughter), physical intimacy (or fireworks), and

11

spiritual intimacy (or oneness). As you move along in the 31 days, more and more of the challenges have to do with sexual technique and spicing things up. And then, at the end, we'll spend a week preparing you to keep that momentum going, even when the 31-day challenge is over.

If you're eager to jump to the "steamy" stuff, please don't. Do the challenges in order. Our biggest sex organ is our brain. We need to *think* the right thoughts about sex and *feel* the right emotions about sex before our bodies will work properly when it comes to sex. The couples who benefited the most from my original self-published version of this book consistently reported that the biggest roadblock isn't technique but communication. One of the biggest breakthroughs they had over the month was finally being able to talk about important aspects of their marriage.

Throughout this 31-day quest, you'll also find a number of "extras." Early in the 31-day challenge, I have an extra challenge for those of you dealing with baggage, hurts, or broken trust, to allow you to hit that reset button on your sex life and move forward. I've also planned three big "pep talks" because sometimes couples need some encouragement and more time to process the challenges. If you have to take a pause, that's okay. A pause may be needed to feel comfortable, especially when sex has been more difficult for one of you than the other. Let the one who is least comfortable set the pace. For sex to be awesome, it has to be mutual. That can't happen if one partner is uncomfortable or scared. In that case, it's better to redo some challenges until you're both on board!

You don't have to get through these challenges in one 31-day calendar month either. I don't know of many couples who have done it all in one month! Most take two to three months, simply because life and work schedules sometimes get in the way. If you want to take a break while she's having her period, by all means do—although many of the challenges don't need to involve intercourse. Play it by ear. There are no hard-and-fast rules.

To keep sex exciting and to give you more ideas and information, you'll also find sidebars that give you extra information, a smorgasbord of new ideas, or some deeper thoughts to chew on. Plus there are some fun ideas to keep things spicy!

While you'll definitely have fireworks this month, often one of the barriers to those fireworks is that you've never sat down and discussed what you want your sex life to be like or what you enjoy or what makes you nervous. That's why many of the challenges are designed to help you take things slow and actually talk about what you're feeling. Taking this opportunity to open those lines of communication will make the physical side of your relationship that much better.

Sex is tied up in our identity, our feelings of self-worth, and our confidence in our marriage. It has the potential to either break you apart or bring you closer than you ever thought you could be. My dream and prayer for each couple reading this is that you will achieve the latter: that you will feel truly intimate and that you will feel as one.

Finally, one last thing you should know before you start. This book is intended for healthy couples who want to work on their sex lives. It is not intended to be used to coerce anyone into things they don't want to do. Additionally, it will not be able to fix an abusive marriage. If sex has become a problem because one spouse is trying to control the other, causing an emotional and sexual rift, that needs to be dealt with. If you're in an abusive marriage, please see the appendix for books that are more appropriate for your situation.

Now let's launch in and have some fun!

DAYS 1–7

Embracing Sex

CATCH THE VISION

Sex is everywhere. It's used to sell shampoo. It's used to sell movies. It motivates clothing purchases, vacation destinations, and even car choices. You can't get away from it.

But what is sex supposed to be about?

As I thought about that question, I browsed the internet for a picture to match the blog post I would write on this topic.[1] I came across a photograph of a man and a woman in their wedding attire: she in a flowing white gown, he in a tuxedo. And they were sitting together on a bed.

I don't know how many of us would have been gutsy enough to have a wedding picture taken on a bed (or how many of us would hang such a picture on our wall), but I think it's refreshing because it says: *This is important. This is a vital part of our relationship. And it all starts now.*

Sex is the physical acting out of everything that marriage is. We become vulnerable with each other. We become completely naked with each other—and that means real intimacy, not just physical intimacy. We cherish each other. We protect each other. But we also have a ton of fun together!

Think about it: in marriage, we are fully committed to each other for life. We laugh together and we cry together. And in sex, we physically demonstrate our commitment to each other and express a range of emotions because sex is uniquely created to do that. God made sex to feel great, but he also made it to be a deeply intimate experience.

While sex is supposed to be stupendous, what if that's not what you're experiencing? What if sex is painful and you can't seem to get it to work at all? What if you've never had anything remotely like the fireworks everyone else talks about? You can't figure out what all the fuss is about, and you're worried that it was created for everyone but you. Or maybe you're haunted by your past—stuff you did breathlessly in the backseat of a car that you can't forget or perhaps something more sinister that was done to you by an uncle or a babysitter or a date. Or maybe you have a hard time staying "present" when you make love—you're haunted by images of porn, movies, or erotica. Intimacy then flies out the window. Or what if sex just feels, well, *blah*, like you're merely going through the motions?

Perhaps you're not going through any motions at all. In surveys I took for my book *The Good Girl's Guide to Great Sex*, I found that 40 percent of couples made love less than once a week. We're just not connecting that often.

This month we're going to walk through these issues and uncover ways to find the true freedom that sex is supposed to be. Though you may struggle with sex, I want you to start this challenge understanding that sex was designed to be wonderful in three ways:

Physically: We're supposed to feel pleasure together.
Emotionally: We're designed to laugh, have fun, and solidify a deep connection.
Spiritually: We're supposed to feel deeply intimate, as if we're truly "one."

Great Sex Challenge 1

Each of you individually, on a scale of 1 to 10 (with 10 being the best), rate your sex life:

Physically _____
Emotionally _____
Spiritually _____

Even if you don't rate all these areas high right now, believe that having all 10s is not only the *potential* for sex but the *intention* for sex—for each of you, and as a couple. You can get there!

Next, wives, say these as a prayer on your own, or just write these words in a journal if you're not religious:

- I believe sex was created to feel great physically and that I am supposed to have a sex drive and supposed to feel aroused, even if I don't feel that way right now.
- I believe sex was created to make me feel loved.
- I believe sex was created to make me feel like one with my husband.

Husbands, say these as a prayer, or just journal them if you're not religious:

- I believe sex was created to feel great physically, not just for me but also for my wife. And I believe God wants me to help her achieve that!
- I believe sex was created to make me feel loved and cherished.
- I believe sex was created to make me feel like one with my wife.

Wrap Up Together

Share with each other how you each rated your sex life. If you have big discrepancies, that isn't a bad thing; you're launching into 31 days together where you're going to grow closer and learn more about making this area of your life great. It's important to start by taking stock, but give each other grace, knowing you're both aiming to grow. If you're both heading in the same direction and are committed to the same goal, it doesn't really matter whether you start at the same place!

Now talk to each other about what a great sex life in each of these three areas would look like for you. What are you aiming for? What would you both like? Again, you don't have to understand how you're going to get there yet. That's around the corner! The important thing is that you see that you were meant to have a great sex life—and that you can.

Whether you have major hang-ups or lots of hurts or fears or doubts, whether your situation is just mediocre, or whether your marriage has scars, sex can be a big positive in your life and in your marriage. See it. Picture it. Believe it! If we start with a positive and enthusiastic attitude about sex, our sex lives will likely improve astronomically. And now, over the next month, we'll look practically at how we're going to make that a reality!

What Sex Means for Each of Us

Billions of people on this planet have had sex. I don't know how many have really made love, because they're not necessarily the same thing.

We tend to think of sex as primarily a physical act. We have sex to feel pleasure. But it's so much more than that. It's a spiritual and emotional intimacy as well—where you feel as if you are truly "one."

Part of that emotional intimacy is evident in how our bodies work.

When a man has sex, the question he's really asking is, *Do you accept me?* He literally enters her body, and in many cases, he leaves part of him behind. When she wants to make love, when she's *eager* to make love, emotionally it feels like she's saying to him, *I accept you, I want you*, even, at its most basic, *We're all good.*

For her, on the other hand, sex is far more physically vulnerable. She allows someone to enter her. What she's asking, then, is *Can I trust you? Do you really love me?* For her to be vulnerable, she first needs to know he is trustworthy.

None of this is to downplay the physical aspects of sex. But the emotional aspects are what make sex much more powerful.

This is why, in general, *men make love to feel loved, whereas women need to feel loved to make love.* He has sex to check on the health of the relationship; she needs the relationship to be healthy before sex can feel intimate to her.

Unfortunately, these differences can easily be a recipe for disaster, prime for misunderstandings!

But there's another way to look at it that I think is part of the bigger design. These two motivators together grow the marriage. If he wants to make love, he needs to woo her so she feels safe. If she wants affection, she needs to respond to him so he feels loved. From these urgings our libidos can grow and expand so that she may also be just as eager to make love and he may also truly want affection! In later challenges we'll look at how libido differences and preferences play out. As we start, though, understanding how your spouse sees sex can not only make sex less confusing but can also point us to how sex was designed to draw us toward real intimacy.

Day 2

CHALLENGING THE LIES
WE BELIEVE ABOUT SEX

Sex may be a beautiful thing, but that doesn't mean we all feel wonderful about it.

What if you're bringing baggage into your marriage that is making it difficult to get excited about sex? Or what if sex has just never felt that great and you've almost given up? Or if it seems impersonal and solely physical?

No matter where you're at today, your sex life can start afresh. But sometimes a fresh start is endangered because we believe things about sex that aren't true. As we're going to learn throughout this month, our primary sex organ is our brain. What we think about sex determines whether we're able to experience deep intimacy and pleasure when we make love. So here's our plan for today: we're going to confront any lies you believe about sex and replace them with truth.

Some of these truths I'm listing are from a Christian perspective. If that's not where you're coming from, fast-forward if you need to. But I'd encourage you to read them because we all need some assurance that we don't have to live with guilt and shame.

You Are a New Creation

Are you haunted by deeds you did before you were married? Do you have flashbacks from old boyfriends or girlfriends—or even an ex-spouse? Are you bothered by past porn use? These things can intrude on your ability to think of sex as something sacred between you and your spouse.

When you have doubts, or when thoughts of your old lovers come back, think about this verse instead: "If anyone is in Christ, the new creation has come: The old has gone, the new is here!" (2 Corinthians 5:17).

You are a new creation. You were bought at a price. You don't have to be that former person anymore, and that old self no longer has claims on you.

Perhaps you don't have much use for the Christian idea of a new creation, but you obviously believe in the institution of marriage because you did walk down that aisle. When we marry, we start afresh. You are now one flesh with your spouse, not with anyone else. The two of you, together, are *also* a new creation. When negative thoughts enter your mind, replace them with the positive: *I am a new creation. We are one flesh, together.*

You Are Pure

When we allow Jesus lordship of our lives, that changes our very nature.[2] When God looks at you, he sees you as pure. Sometimes we have difficulty feeling like we're new creations because we know what we've done in the past. Other times we have difficulties because of what was done to us. We were abused or raped or fondled or harassed. And we feel like we're tainted, used, and dirty.

That is not the way God sees his children. God does not judge you in terms of what others did to you; he sees you only in terms of what Jesus did for you. You are completely and utterly pure once you follow him.

The next time you feel dirty because of what was done to you, the next time you think everyone else is healthy but you never will be, the next time you feel like there is no hope for you, remember this verse: "He . . . will rejoice over you with singing" (Zephaniah 3:17).

Think of how a parent holds a baby and sings to them, so amazed at how precious they are. That is how God thinks of you. He rejoices over you!

You Were Created for Pleasure

You were made to feel sexual pleasure. Men usually have an easier time believing this because they tend to be guaranteed pleasure when they make love. In fact, that's what usually ends a sexual encounter—when he reaches orgasm. But women were also created for pleasure, and I can prove it.

If you're a woman, you have a clitoris, a little knob of flesh just in front of your vagina that has no other purpose except to bring pleasure. Guys don't have that. Their primary sexual organ is multifunctional. But God put more nerve endings in the clitoris than he did in the entire penis! God gave women a little piece of our bodies that was made simply to feel good—very good.

If you're a woman and sex doesn't feel great for you and you believe, "I will never have an orgasm," or "I can't see what all the fuss is about," or "Everyone else may like sex, but I never will," stop it. Instead, say, "*I was created to feel pleasure.*"

It's true. And wouldn't you rather say something to yourself that's true than keep believing a lie?

Some women reading this may not have experienced a lot of pleasure before. That's okay. In the surveys I took for my book *The Good Girl's Guide to Great Sex*, I found that the best years for sexual pleasure for married women are sixteen to twenty-four years into the marriage. If you've been married only for a short while, know this: women get more orgasmic with time and practice. So instead of doubting or worrying or giving up, get excited!

A word to husbands: perhaps you doubt whether your wife can ever feel pleasure. You need to believe this truth as well: *She was created to feel pleasure.* Her body is capable of it. You just need to learn how to both get in the right frame of mind, how to nurture your relationship, and then how to move together physically. That may sound like a tall order, but it's a fun one. And it is not just possible; with the right frame of mind, it's probable!

You Were Created for Intimacy

Not only were we created to feel wonderful during sex; we were also created to be intimate. Sex is supposed to unite us together not only with our genitals but also with our hearts. Unfortunately, sex often becomes more pornographic than intimate. When we think of sex, we think of something almost impersonal. The idea of what our bodies are doing is sexy, not the idea of whom we're doing it with.

That's a result of living in our society. We've taken sex out of the context of marriage, and so it's become only physical. When you get married, it's hard to make that mental switch so that sex becomes something so much more than just physical. Pornography just adds to the confusion.

If you're wondering whether you'll ever be able to feel love, and not just arousal, when it comes to the bedroom, then repeat this to yourself: *"I was created for intimacy."*

During this month I'm going to give you tools to experience that!

Sex Is Beautiful

Sex is rather awkward. It's messy. You're all sweaty, and there's stuff to clean up afterward. And sometimes it just doesn't seem, well, *proper.* It's all too easy for many of us to think, "Sex is something we have to do to make babies, but it's best not to dwell on it too much." Women, especially, like feeling in control, clean, and organized. Sex doesn't fit into that mold.

Maybe it's time to throw out the mold. Sex is supposed to be a little messy. Sex is supposed to make you vulnerable and a bit out of control. It's not supposed to be clinical!

Some of us were raised to think sex was something never to be spoken of or thought of, and then when we got married, the transition to seeing sex as something beautiful was hard to make. We still wonder whether there really is something dirty or wrong with the whole thing.

That is another lie holding you and your marriage back. When God finished creating Adam and Eve, he pronounced them—naked as jaybirds—"very good" (Genesis 1:31). Sex is very good. If you start doubting it, repeat over and over: *"Sex is beautiful. Sex is very good."*

Sex Benefits You

Finally, here's the most common destructive view of sex: many of us have come to see sex as an obligation. When we think about sex, we tend to think, "Do I have to tonight?" We figure we *should* because our spouses need it. If you're the spouse with the lower libido, you probably have come to see sex as one more thing on your to-do list. And when you don't do it, your spouse can get irritated—hardly a sexy thought.

But sex helps you too! If you're really tired, sex will help you get to sleep faster and sleep more deeply. If you're anxious, making love will help calm you down. Making love boosts your immunity, makes you less depressed, and best of all, makes you feel far more connected to your spouse.[3]

Next time you think, "I guess I have to tonight, even if I don't want to," stop yourself, and replace it with this: "Sex benefits *me*."

I know many of you would like to move on to the nitty-gritty of sex, but don't worry. We're going to get there soon! But before we can work at making the practicalities of sex work wonderfully, we need to make sure we hold the right beliefs about sex. Sex isn't magically going to work if you're still walking around feeling slightly dirty, embarrassed, guilty, or obligated. We need to get our heads in the game because when our heads aren't there, our bodies won't follow.

Great Sex Challenge 2

Part A

Take turns answering this question: Of all the truths listed above, which do you have the most trouble believing?

Have you given up hope that sex will ever feel good for you—or for your spouse? Do you still feel like sex is a little creepy or wrong? Or do you see it mostly in pornographic rather than intimate terms? Do you see sex as an obligation? Talk about your roadblocks, and then talk about strategies you can work on together so that when you slip into a pattern of believing lies, your spouse can help you.

For instance, if your spouse has difficulty believing that sex can feel good, ask her (or him), when you start feeling hopeless, "What can I do to help redirect you?" or "You are created for pleasure, and one day we will get there, I promise," or "You are beautiful to me, and I love you, and you are meant for so much more." Alternatively, if he has trouble believing that one day he will feel like sex is intimate, rather than just pornographic, she could say, "You show me every day in little ways that you love me. You were created to love me in bed, and I know we will get there."

Talk about which affirmations would be most effective to combat the top lies you each struggle with and then start practicing them.

Part B

Each of you share two memories from your childhood/teenage years that have to do with sex or puberty—one negative memory and one positive memory. When did you feel shame? When did you feel proud or grown up or excited? Then talk about how these experiences shaped your view of sex.

When you're finished, practice using your new affirmations again. You've got this! No matter what lies you grew up believing, together you're going to take these next four weeks to work at truly giving yourselves a fresh, exciting new start.

For Those Dealing with Sexual Baggage: Do You Need a Reset Button on Your Sex Life?

Some of you working through this book are doing so because you want to spice things up, get out of a rut, or learn how to talk about sex with each other more freely. But some of you have some much deeper issues—sexual baggage from the past that still haunts you: past affairs, porn use, or something else that has broken trust between you or wounded you in the past.

If you're doing this challenge just to spice things up, feel free to proceed to day 3!

But if you've got baggage, it's much better to work through this extra challenge first. Great sex requires vulnerability, and this 31-day challenge requires vulnerability. But you can't be vulnerable if there are trust issues in your marriage or if you have baggage you haven't unpacked, especially in your sex life. So let's deal with those issues tonight!

Do you need a reset button for your sex life?

Some of us have trunkloads of sexual baggage—whether it's lies we've believed or abuse we've suffered or even things we've done that we're not proud of. Maybe you had some sexual partners before you were married, and you wish you could get them out of your head. Maybe one or both of you were into porn. Maybe you have a hard time getting over what you know your spouse did before you were married.

Today we're going to symbolically hit the reset button on your sex life. Once you've dealt with your past, what went on before doesn't need to doom your sex life now.

EMBRACE YOUR NEW IDENTITY

In Genesis 2:24 God said, "A man leaves his father and mother and is united to his wife, and they become one flesh." When you married your spouse, you became something new, no longer defined by what went on before.

This truth can be difficult to accept, especially if you have been hurt sexually in the past through abuse or sexual assault. For many people, sex seems dirty, and seeing it as something beautiful and new seems impossible. But I don't believe God wants you to allow that person, or those people, to rob you of the abundant life and abundant marriage he prepared for you. He wants you to achieve healing! So pray with your spouse that you will be able to see sex as very different today than it was then. Make an appointment to talk to a licensed counselor if this is a long-standing problem, because we aren't meant to deal with problems alone. A counselor who is trained in trauma therapy can guide you through the healing process that God wants for you.

FORGIVE EACH OTHER

Sometimes our problems don't predate marriage. We messed up *after* we walked down the aisle. Someone broke trust through a physical affair, an emotional affair, or pornography use. This book is meant to help two committed spouses grow their sex life. If trust is currently being broken through porn use or affairs, please stop this study and take steps to heal your relationship before you resume. You can't build a good sex life without trust.

If these infractions were in the past, how do you move forward? Before healing can occur, the offending spouse must take full ownership of what they did, understanding the severity of it. It is not enough to say, "I used to use porn a lot, but I promise not to again. Just please don't tell anyone else about it." You also shouldn't say, "I broke it off with him, and now you have to forgive me." If you wounded your spouse, it's your responsibility to rebuild trust, not to demand instant forgiveness.

First seek out an accountability partner or join a recovery group. We aren't meant to struggle through this life alone. If you have been tempted by porn or had an emotional affair or an actual affair, you need a same-sex accountability partner. You don't have to tell everyone under the sun, but telling one person is a way to show your spouse that you're serious about changing and moving on. Then set up an appointment to see a licensed counselor, both individually and together. Break off all contact with any third parties, and get filters or controls on your devices. Be transparent by sharing passwords and computer access.

Once the offending spouse has taken these steps, the ball is now in the other spouse's court. If your spouse has broken trust, at some point you will have to forgive if you want to move on. That amount of time should be commensurate with the degree of the damage. It's unwise not to give time to heal. Don't rush it.

But delaying healing isn't wise either. Unfair or not, there is nothing your spouse can do to make it up to you. You will never achieve true intimacy until you extend forgiveness. Once your spouse has set up accountability systems and has shown over time that they are trustworthy, it is now up to you to forgive and move forward.

TAKE EVERY THOUGHT CAPTIVE

Part of moving on is deciding that you will no longer dwell on what came before. We don't have to entertain every thought that comes into our heads. The Bible challenges us to "take every thought captive" (2 Corinthians 10:5 NRSV), which means that when a thought enters your head, you can look at it, decide whether you want to entertain it, and then discard it if you think it's hurting you. If a thought isn't true or doesn't help, you don't have to dwell on it.

If you're haunted by memories of abuse, learn to reject those thoughts (a licensed counselor trained in trauma therapy can help you do this). If you're haunted by thoughts of what your spouse has done, learn how to throw those out too. You don't have to rehash everything multiple times. That also means you don't need to know in detail everything your spouse did. Asking for specifics about your spouse's past sexual exploits so that you have more vivid visual pictures won't help, and it will also hurt your spouse as they try to move forward.

What may help you, especially if you're haunted by what your spouse did before you were married (or after you were married), is to affirm this truth: *Making love is not a matter of understanding everything about sex; it's understanding everything about each other. And it's about how two people work together. What we have is unique and beautiful and doesn't warrant being compared with anything else.*

Even if your spouse was married previously and you worry that you're being compared, remember that what you have together is unique because you both are unique. That's a good thing! Don't focus on "Did he enjoy it more before?" or "Did she like it better with him?" Focus on "We are unique and beautiful together."

HIT THAT RESET BUTTON!

Reassure your spouse that they are the sole object of your desire; agree you will not dwell on any past partners or on porn. Then pray together through your reset. Ask for forgiveness if you need to, and offer forgiveness if you need to. Thank God that you are both new creations and "one flesh" now.

Now here's the fun part: plan a special dinner where you commit to starting over. Then make your reset visible! Buy new bedding. Change the position of the bed in your bedroom. Buy new candles or pillows. Do something different so that you can see "we are different now."

It may even help to add some humor to this struggle by getting a "buzzer" you can hit whenever past hurts or baggage intrude on your thoughts. Some board games, such as Taboo, have buzzers. Keep one in your bedside table. From now on, if you feel antsy and like you're being drawn back into old arguments, suspicions, or hurts, dig out that buzzer and say, "I need to hit this reset button again!" Then hit it, shake it off, laugh, and start again.

For Couples Dealing with Porn: 6 Things You Must Do

If one or both of you use porn, that must stop. No ifs, ands, or buts. Porn fuels sex trafficking and hurts real people. It rewires the brain so that what's arousing is an image or a video rather than a person, and it wrecks intimacy. It can't be tolerated in a committed, loving relationship. Here, then, is a snapshot of a game plan to defeat it.

1. Bring it to light.

If your spouse uses porn and will not talk to anyone about it—and will not let you talk to anyone about it—your spouse is not dedicated to change. Real repentance should be accompanied by confession to others. If your spouse insists on hiding their phone or computer, then bring a friend, mentor, pastor, counselor, or someone else they respect to talk to them with you and say, "This will no longer be tolerated."

2. Identify your triggers.

For the porn user: When are you most likely to turn to porn? Is it because of boredom? Stress? Anger? Feeling distant from your spouse? Make a game plan to reduce those triggers, and brainstorm a list of alternative activities you will do when negative feelings occur. For instance, if the pull to porn is highest when you're bored, start reading and have books throughout the house. Start an indoor hobby you can easily turn to that does not involve a screen, such as doing puzzles, painting, working out, or cooking. If stress is a trigger, start an exercise program or an outdoor hobby, like walking, biking, or birding, or pencil in more time with friends who rejuvenate you.

3. Get blockers on your computer/phone/devices.

Set up blockers on your devices. Filters won't cure a porn addiction, but they do lower temptation. If you have to go through obstacles to access porn, it's more likely you'll remember that you want to change, listen to the Holy Spirit's voice, and stop. This is the equivalent to an alcoholic clearing the house of alcohol. It doesn't end the addiction, but it does make it harder to fulfill that temptation, and so sets the stage for healing.

4. Seek accountability and counseling.

Porn use often grows from deep emotional scars, and then the porn use itself produces its own scars. Users can benefit from counseling. Emotional development often stops at the point when porn use starts, because users turn to porn as a coping mechanism when they experience anything negative. Because of that habit, many porn users never learn to properly deal with negative emotions. Through counseling and recovery groups, some of these scars can be healed, which will also reduce the pull of porn.

5. Recover from setbacks.

Many recovering porn users do fall. They may be clean for a few months, or even a few years, and then stress happens or a trigger pops up, and they turn to porn for a time. When this happens, confess, apologize, but don't despair. Identify the triggers, address them, and take actions that make future setbacks less likely.

6. Fight the porn, not each other.

When a woman hears that her husband has been watching porn, she will often feel violated, betrayed, even disgusted. It's important for her to have time to process this and maybe even see a counselor as well. But if the husband (or wife, if she's the porn user) is committed to quitting and is seeking help, then try to fight the porn together rather than fighting each other. Help each other minimize triggers. Pray for each other. Try not to view your spouse through the lens of porn, but keep encouraging and affirming each other. You can get through this; so many couples have. And Jesus loves to bring that which was damaged and broken back to wholeness!

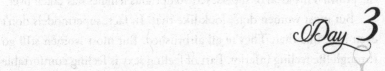

EMBRACE THE SKIN SHE'S IN

Women, are you beautiful?

Even contemplating the answer to that question has probably heaped a whole pile of guilt at your feet. You feel ugly. You feel too big. You don't measure up.

And guys, you may look at your wife and think she's beautiful, but I can practically guarantee that she doesn't think so. Everywhere she turns she sees images that say she'll never be enough. When we women feel unattractive, we feel distinctly unsexy. Today's challenge is about helping her celebrate the skin she's in!

Let's look first at the root of the problem. Women the world over have a far greater desire to be beautiful than men do. Some of this is likely innate, and some is likely because our culture judges women on beauty far more than it does men. Whatever the cause, women want to be attractive. Add to that our culture's obsession with sex, and beauty takes on an even more exaggerated importance. When sex is taken outside of marriage, as our culture has done, the drive for intimacy is replaced with merely a physical drive, elevating the physical aspects of sex even more. All you have left, then, is physical attraction. "Sexiness" becomes of vital importance. Even if other aspects of sex matter to us, our culture's obsession with sexiness still affects us. It's like it's in the water. We can't escape it.

Picture the covers of *Maxim* and *Cosmopolitan*, for instance. *Maxim* is for men and *Cosmo* for women, but other than that they're pretty much the same. Both feature seminaked women looking as if they're on the prowl. This ideal of supersexed voluptuous females has taken over.

But most women don't look like that. In fact, supermodels don't even look like that. They're all airbrushed. But most women still go through life feeling inferior. Part of feeling sexy is feeling comfortable in your own skin, and many women are so embarrassed and ashamed of their bodies that they do their utmost not to think about them. We hide them in oversized clothes. We try to ignore them because anything that reminds us of our physical bodies also reminds us that we're inadequate. That's why we women often become quite dissociated from our bodies. And when we're dissociated from them, it's awfully hard to get in the mood!

One of the most frustrating things for my husband was when he would proposition me, and I would reply, "I just don't feel attractive." His response: "If I want you, you are, by definition, attractive!" He was attracted to me. But I didn't feel attractive. It's a common frustration couples face. So let me talk directly to each of you today.

Note for Women

Given that supermodels are photoshopped and that our whole culture's emphasis on beauty is overkill, are we going to allow our culture to set our sexual self-esteem? Are we going to allow our culture to make us feel ugly—and rob us of the pleasure we're supposed to feel in marriage? Ladies, if you're like me, you're tired of the media's negative messages about how we should look. So let's reject those messages!

Tell yourself:

I will not let our culture dictate how I think about my body. I was designed for pleasure—no matter what I look like—and I am going to allow myself to feel it!

Ironically, as you embrace your body and accept it, taking care of it becomes easier. Women with more self-confidence have an easier time losing weight. In one study, women who were coached to have better body image lost an average of 7 percent of their body weight on their weight loss regimen, while the control group lost only 2 percent.[4] If you are packing an extra sixty or eighty pounds, the answer isn't to berate yourself about it. Embrace your body and have as much fun with it as you can. Love your body, and you'll treat it better.

Note for Men

Now a word to you men. Many, if not most, of you love and appreciate your wife's body and wish she could see it as you do. Your challenge today will work toward this.

But then there are husbands who are more critical. I receive many emails from women who say to me, "My husband is upset that my body doesn't look like it did before I had kids. He tells me that he's not attracted to me anymore. He doesn't want to hurt me, but he feels like he should be honest. But I just can't lose the weight. What do I do?"

Maybe your wife has gained some weight. She probably doesn't look like the women in movies or in magazines (although those women don't look like that either). Here are your choices: you can further demoralize her and wreck her self-esteem, which will cause her to flee from sex even more; or you can embrace her, show her you love her, show her you want to have a great time with her, and boost her self-esteem. Studies show that women who appreciate their bodies have a much easier time losing weight than women who feel lousy about their bodies. Your choice matters.

Today your goal is to help her feel beautiful. That means you need to commit to letting her be the beauty in your life. Your eyes must be entirely for her. Like Proverbs says, "May her breasts satisfy you at all times" (Proverbs 5:19 NRSV). This isn't directed at women— *make sure you stay in shape so you're always pretty!* This is directed at men—"Rejoice in the wife of your youth" (Proverbs 5:18). And it's a command!

You are in a unique position to help your wife get over her insecurities and embrace her body. Will you do it?

Great Sex Challenge 3

PART 1

Both of you, separately, list five features that you like best about her body. Get a pen and paper and write them down, or jot them on your phone. Women, you must name five! Listing three or four isn't good enough. All of us can name five we hate; today name five you love. And don't ask your husband for help! It's important that you yourself learn to enjoy your body.

PART 2

Once you each have your five, share them with each other like this:

Have her share each of the five with him. As she shares them, have him pay special attention to each one. He can touch, caress, kiss, whatever. You can do this with her naked, or you can slowly undress her as she shares. Whatever makes her feel the most comfortable!

Bonus: To make this one spicier, if she's comfortable, have her show which ones she enjoys! Ladies, if you're proud of your breasts, go into the bathroom, get undressed, and come out wearing nothing but a long dangly necklace. Like your hips? Draw a little heart tattoo with a lip pencil. Or you can do this throughout the week to remind yourself of the parts of you that you like. Like your feet? Paint your toenails!

After she's shared her favorite parts, it's his turn to reveal his. Men, you can touch each one you like. Linger there a bit. Kiss, touch, nibble, anything! Tell her how much you like each part and what's so appealing about it before moving on to the next. And you must pay attention to all five before you do anything else in bed tonight!

8 Ways Hollywood Wrecks Our Expectations of Sex

1. She looks like a supermodel.

According to network television, forensic scientists are drop-dead gorgeous and always arrive at crime scenes in heels and with perfect eye shadow. Everybody in Hollywood looks perfect. But look around at the people you know in real life. We aren't that beautiful of a bunch. Most of us look pretty normal.

What We Feel: It's easy to think you can't be sexy if you don't match the stars on the screen. Hollywood tells us that flawless is sexy. So if we have flaws, we figure we aren't sexy. And when we don't feel sexy, we often shut down. Don't let Hollywood shut you down! Hollywood's not worth it.

2. He looks like an Adonis.

Hollywood doesn't only portray unrealistic women; every man in Hollywood has a six-pack. And they don't age either! I remember watching the sixties movie *To Kill a Mockingbird*. Gregory Peck, who played Atticus Finch, was forty-six years old when he acted in it, and he looked like a forty-six-year-old. We watched it in 2011, when Brad Pitt was forty-eight and graced almost every magazine cover in the checkout line. But Brad Pitt easily looked fifteen years younger.

What We Feel: Men aren't supposed to be distinguished anymore; they're supposed to be sexy. That can warp how women see and feel attraction toward their husbands and can cause men to join the insecurity club.

3. Women always have libidos through the roof.

Women want sex all the time, just as much as men do. Whole shows are dedicated to this myth: *Sex and the City*, *Jersey Shore*. Women are on the prowl.

What We Feel: If women watch these shows long enough, they may worry that they're frigid. If you're not on the prowl, are you undersexed? Nope. Most women's desire and arousal don't kick in until they've started to make love. While some women have high sex drives, many women just don't. But that doesn't mean you can't enjoy making love! If you throw yourself into it and believe that your body will follow, it likely will. If, on the other hand, you believe Hollywood and you wait until you're completely turned on to have sex, you may be waiting a long time.

4. Men always have libidos through the roof.

Men are sex obsessed. Every man is thinking about sex all the time. Whether it's the nerds in *The Big Bang Theory* or the lawyers from *Suits*, they're all out to "get some."

What We Feel: According to my survey for *The Good Girl's Guide to Great Sex*, about 24 percent of women have the higher sex drive in their marriage. For those women, the logical conclusion seems to be "I must be really, really undesirable. Every other guy is sex obsessed except for mine!" But what if it's not true? What if not every guy *is* sex obsessed? If your husband doesn't want sex as much as you do, you're not alone, and you're not a freak.

5. Porn is fun. (Not!)

When characters on sitcoms watch porn, it's usually something to laugh about. Sometimes couples watch it together in the hopes of getting aroused together. Or the guys watch porn on poker night. It's a natural part of life.

What We Feel: Men may figure porn is a harmless endeavor. Then when a husband watches porn and tells his wife, "Everybody does it," she wonders, "Am I a prude for thinking this is wrong?" Porn wrecks marriages. Porn isn't harmless. It causes people to fantasize, to dissociate, and not to be able to achieve arousal by a person but only by an image. It causes people to turn to porn instead of each other and soon takes away desire for one's spouse almost entirely. It's selfish. And it's exploitative. A marriage will steadily go downhill if one or both partners watch porn, which is likely why porn use doubles the chance of divorce.[5]

6. Marriage is boring.

Back in the 1990s my husband and I watched *Friends*. Chandler's humor matched ours and we loved him. But one night, after a particularly raunchy episode, we realized we were essentially watching a show about people jumping into bed with one another. And we stopped watching.

In Hollywood, the hottest sex scenes usually occur the first time a couple falls into bed. The conquest makes it so alluring. Most shows, then, revolve around winning a new person to have sex with. Marriage, when you're past that "first" time decades ago, seems awfully boring in comparison.

What We Feel: Sex should always be new, fresh, and exciting, but sometimes marriage is the opposite of all that. We feel like we're missing out on something and all we have is the boring leftovers. The reason we're not satisfied, we think, must be because we're with the same partner who doesn't know how to turn us on. In reality, the best sex is between married people—and not even newlyweds! (Remember what I said about the best sex being in years sixteen to twenty-four?) Married sex isn't boring—commitment is actually far sexier than conquests!

7. Foreplay is unnecessary.

Most women require plenty of foreplay to become aroused enough to enjoy making love. And many women require a lot of touching to reach climax. On the screen, though, people grope and kiss, and within less than two minutes, the clothes are off and the bodies are joined. No one ever gropes around to find just the right body parts to caress. No one ever has to ask, "Is this the right place?" They automatically know, and everyone immediately experiences magnificent sex.

What We Feel: If simply ripping off clothes isn't enough to arouse us, we wonder if something is wrong. Women may feel weird and uncomfortable asking our husbands for more foreplay because it honestly looks like *no one else needs it*. Women think everyone else must be way more sexually responsive than we are because two minutes of groping does nothing for us. Men too think foreplay is highly overrated because it's rarely portrayed. To both spouses it can seem like something is wrong with the wife if she needs more warming up.

8. The couple always reaches the big "O" simultaneously.

No one ever struggles with making sex feel good. From the first time (in movies like *The Notebook*), women experience absolute bliss. And the bliss is perfectly timed too! There's no "making sure she feels good" first. There's no struggling with how to reach the big "O" at all! It's ridiculously easy and natural.

What We Feel: No wonder so many new brides feel like there's something wrong with their bodies! Most women don't experience automatic orgasm. They don't. That's not to say it isn't possible, but it isn't terribly common. In my surveys for *The Good Girl's Guide to Great Sex*, only about 61 percent of women "usually" or "always" experienced orgasm when they had sex, and sometimes that wasn't even through intercourse. It's great to aim for the stars, but you're not failing as a couple if orgasm doesn't happen easily.

Women's bodies were made to take longer to heat up. Women's bodies were made in a way that for sex to feel good for both of you, you have to have a lot of communication. You have to know each other well. You have to be vulnerable. Orgasm isn't automatic, and that's perfectly okay.

It is not *you* who's messed up when it comes to sex; it's Hollywood!

So don't look at Hollywood as the baseline for what your sex life should be. And don't worry what other people are experiencing either. What matters is what you both experience together. Let's move forward in discovering how to make that experience amazing.

Day 4

PUCKER UP!

Do you remember your dreams of a first kiss? You watched all those after-school specials on TV, and you could hardly wait until it happened to you. You pictured it. You practiced it in your mind. You imagined whom it would be with. And in those heady days when you were prepubescent, kissing was likely as far as those fantasies went.

And then, for so many couples, you got married, and kissing almost came to a halt.

I think it's because of a misunderstanding of what kissing is for. Many husbands, for instance, often think kissing is foreplay—as in, it's necessarily going somewhere. And because many women are reluctant to put a down payment on something they may not want to purchase later, so to speak, they stop kissing so that he doesn't get the wrong idea.

Kissing then becomes something she may actively avoid unless you're about to have sex. And he may avoid it too, thinking it's not necessary except in the bedroom. But that's too bad because kissing makes women feel closer to our men! It's fun. It's intimate. And it grosses out the kids (in a good way).

Just because you're not sure you're going to want to make love in the evening is no reason to avoid kissing earlier in the day (now, if one of you always turns down the other, that's a problem, but we'll get to that later this month). If you avoid kissing, then women especially are deprived of one of our primary ways to get our libidos up—and almost guarantee she *won't* want to make love later.

Most couples kiss only as foreplay—not for affection throughout the day. Or if they do kiss, it's just a quick peck. So I want you to start kissing—really kissing—every day!

QUICK KISSING TIPS

- Saliva: some like it; some don't. Find out your spouse's preference (and tell your spouse yours!).
- Tongue: Same thing. Some really like it. Some don't. Keep it light! If your spouse is too tongue-happy, say, "Let me kiss you for thirty seconds and show you how I like it." Then do so enthusiastically!
- Breath mints are your friend. Have some in your purse, and use them throughout the day. Toothbrushes are your friend too!
- Use your hands. Caress your spouse's back, arms, head, or wherever you like.
- Savor it. Especially to the men: don't rush to turn kissing into something else. The romance of kissing will rev her engines. If you hurry things and start groping her or touching her breasts every time you kiss, chances are you'll turn her off. Think of kissing like an amazing appetizer before a meal. You don't gorge it down so you can get to the meal; you enjoy it for itself. So just kiss her! It helps her feel loved and wanted.

Great Sex Challenge 4

Set the kitchen timer, and kiss for at least fifteen seconds. It's amazing how long fifteen seconds seems. Repeat this every day (and not just at night while you're lying in bed). You'll feel warmer toward your spouse, and sex will feel more intimate.

Day 5

Awaken Her Body

Many women don't like their bodies, and because of that, we're often disconnected from them. But if we're disconnected from our bodies, we aren't going to feel a whole lot of pleasure.

That disconnect could be because we feel embarrassed about our bodies or embarrassed about sex in general. It could be because you as a couple have never figured out how to make sex feel good. And it could be because she's starting to doubt whether she *can* feel good.

Today we're going to focus on reassuring her that her body can indeed feel pleasure and showing him that he can actually provide it. While people in movies may grope each other and then quickly fall into bed in rapturous pleasure, most women don't work that way. They take far more time.

For those of you who have seen *The Notebook*, you'll know that Allie, who's a virgin, has the best sex ever her first time out the gate. She makes mad passionate love with Noah, and everything goes so amazingly wonderfully—including an earth-shattering climax.

Women watch that sort of thing and think, "That's what sex is like for everyone but me. I'm a freak. I have to work so hard to feel aroused, and I'm not even sure that I can get aroused. It will never work for me." Men watch that and may think, "What's wrong with my wife? Why doesn't she respond like that?"

Hold it right there.

Remember day 2, when we talked about some of the lies we believe? One of the most common lies for women is "I will never feel pleasure." It's not true.

I often wish I could take couples back in time to before the wedding night, or before they had sex for the first time, and say, "Instead of aiming for sex, *aim for arousal.*" Make sure she feels good, regardless of whether sex happens. Instead, we do the opposite. We have sex regardless of whether arousal happens. And that can cement in her mind: "I just don't enjoy this very much." And it can cement in his mind: "Intercourse is what matters, so the rest isn't as important."

Let's change all that today!

Women were made with a body part specifically designed to feel pleasure—and we're going to talk about the clitoris more throughout the month. But just because women have that little body part does not mean it gets stimulated enough in a few minutes to make sex wonderful.

Instead, here's what happens with so many couples:

He fumbles a bit trying to make her feel good, but he may not know the right way to touch her because men and women like to be touched differently. Men tend to like a firm touch; women tend to like it much more lightly. If a man touches a woman the way he wants to be touched, it's not going to be pleasurable.

He may touch her a little too firmly, raptures don't follow, but she's too embarrassed to speak up. She thinks, "I guess I just don't like my breasts touched," or "I guess I'm just not sensitive."

She grows increasingly anxious about why she's not feeling pleasure, so she tries to force some pleasurable feelings. That just compounds the problem because when we're anxious, we can't relax, and when we can't relax, we don't feel arousal very easily.

Are you in that vicious cycle? Maybe you're not, and you're here for tips on how to make sex even more stupendous. It's okay right now, but you'd like to ramp it up. That's wonderful, and I think you'll get a lot out of this month!

But some couples have serious problems in the bedroom, and going through these 31 days is a difficult process. I received this email when I worked through this series on my blog:

> Sex has long been a really, really hard part of my marriage since we got married. No matter what we've tried—it's not getting better. It's worse. Yesterday's blog post about lies was painful. It felt like you'd listened in on my internal monologue and aired it to everyone. I was really upset—and thankful.
>
> I might have to make cue cards to remind me of the truths you shared.
>
> I asked hubby to do this [series] with me. He jumped at the chance—because he knows how much of a struggle this is with me. And tonight we started.
>
> Wow—we haven't talked like that in so long. It was amazing. Although we have a long way to go, thank you for making it possible for us to open the lines of communication.
>
> Tonight, I want to cry because I feel like maybe, just maybe, there's hope I'll become the woman that God intends me to be, the woman that my DH [dear husband] prayed for, the woman I should be.

Today I want to give you a challenge that will hopefully give both of you even more confidence and encouragement.

Great Sex Challenge 5

Light some candles, get a space heater or a fan to make sure your bedroom is comfortable, and get out some massage oil. Now take a timer and set it for fifteen minutes. For the next fifteen minutes, while she lies still, he will explore her body, without any expectation that she will orgasm. And you can't make love! This isn't foreplay. This is just *play*. Now some special direction for both of you:

CHALLENGE FOR HER

- If he's too rough, tell him gently (or take his hand and show him how to do it better).
- If something gives you the willies (if you have anxiety from previous abuse, for instance), ask him to move on to a different body part. And if you need to take a time-out, that's okay too. But try to let him keep touching you, even if it's only in "safe" places.
- Do your utmost to concentrate on what he's doing. Don't worry about the timer. Don't worry whether he's grossed out or whether he doesn't want to do this or whether he thinks this is silly. Instead, pay attention to your body. Ask yourself, "What wants to be touched now?" When you ask yourself that question, you may just realize you *do* want to be touched!
- Don't worry about having an orgasm! Honestly. Sometimes the reason we can't experience pleasure is because we get too goal-oriented. Just relax and treat this attention like a gift.
- Since he's probably going to be pretty worked up, you can always make love afterward if you'd like. Give him the gift of not having to worry about your feeling good. The purpose here is to get away from anything goal-oriented and just to learn that your body can indeed feel pleasure. That's easier to do when there's no pressure and when you're relaxed!
- It could be that you're really nervous and have a hard time relaxing during those fifteen minutes. Try it in the bathtub if that's easier. And if this first time doesn't go well, don't fret. Sometimes we need to repeat this exercise a few times before we feel good. Use lots of massage oil, and if you're nervous, encourage your husband to concentrate on your legs and back, only slowly working his way to your traditional erogenous zones. The goal is to learn to relax and just to *feel*.

CHALLENGE FOR HIM

- Start slowly. Don't go straight for her breasts or her clitoris. Rub her back or the backs of her thighs. It's usually much more arousing if you build up to something than if you launch straight in, especially if she's anxious.

- Don't let her turn this into something for you! If she's nervous about feeling good or about getting all this attention, she may try to say, "That's enough—now let's make love!" Don't give in. Give her the full fifteen minutes. Many women are embarrassed or scared to let their bodies truly feel. Many women are embarrassed to be the center of attention, which is a huge roadblock to embracing their sexuality. Give your wife this gift.

- This is the hardest part: agree in your heart and mind before you start that this may not go anywhere else. She *may* want to make love afterward, but the best gift you can give her is to say, "There are no expectations. I want this to be for you." Then touch her without expecting or demanding anything else. For so many women, sex has become an obligation, and that is *not* sexy. The purpose of this exercise is to help her see that her body can experience pleasure. If you turn this into an obligation, she may not be able to relax enough to feel aroused. And don't worry; your turn is coming! But let tonight be her gift and her awakening, even if it's a little frustrating for you.

10 Things You Might Not Know about Women and Arousal

While we're quite familiar with what arousal looks like for men (it's so visible, after all!), women's arousal can be more of a mystery. Here are ten things you may not know.

1. Women have erections too.

The main sign of a man's arousal is an erect penis, which is awfully hard to miss (though there are other signs as well). But men aren't the only ones who grow with arousal. The clitoris can grow from around three to four millimeters in height to around eight millimeters (though some women may grow much larger). When the clitoris becomes erect, blood flow increases to the genitals, and the vulva becomes engorged to make penetration easier.

2. Women have several physiological signs of arousal.

Clitoral erection and genital engorgement aren't the only signs of arousal. Women's nipples become erect, and the areola (the darker part around the nipple) can swell by up to 25 percent. The pupils will often dilate (hence "bedroom eyes"), and she'll tend to breathe faster and feel flushed.

3. Before orgasm, the clitoris retracts into the hood to avoid direct stimulation.

After the arousal period, women will experience what is called "sexual plateau," when the body is getting ready for orgasm. She usually requires stimulation to push her over the edge. During sexual plateau, engorgement will continue, but the clitoris will look less erect because it will retract into the clitoral hood—so it appears almost "flat" against the body. It becomes less about stimulating her directly and more about rubbing against the whole region. Many researchers believe the clitoral "roots" extend up into the vaginal wall and form what we know as the

G-spot. As he contacts the pubic bone during intercourse, it stimulates the whole region and even the interior vaginal wall.

4. Women have several erogenous zones that can lead to arousal. Some of these zones are more powerful than others, but the ears, neck, mouth, backs of knees, inner thighs, and inside of the arms can be erogenous zones. So can toes (if you're not overly ticklish!). We tend to think of the breasts and the clitoris as the most important erogenous zones, but when trying to get your wife aroused, it's often better to warm up with other areas first to help calm her mind, settle in, and look forward to what's next. Starting right away with the clitoris can be overpowering for some women. Especially for women with sexual abuse in their past, warming up with other erogenous zones, or even with a massage, can help overcome flashbacks or negative connotations.

5. Women's sexual response cycle is different from men's. Men's sexual response cycle usually looks like this:

DESIRE (LIBIDO) → AROUSAL (EXCITEMENT) → ORGASM → RESOLUTION

For women it can look a little different:

AROUSAL (EXCITEMENT) → DESIRE (LIBIDO) → ORGASM → RESOLUTION

Some women feel desire for sex first, but for many, the feeling that they actually want sex doesn't kick in until stimulation—and arousal—has begun. Women tend to be responsive when it comes to arousal and desire, meaning that we tend to respond to stimulation rather than feeling something on our own beforehand.

6. Sometimes (but not always), arousal can be impossible, no matter what stimulation is being provided, if her brain is not "into it."

Though desire often follows arousal, this doesn't mean that women automatically get aroused with stimulation. It can happen (more on that in a second), but often women's brains have to be positively engaged, or arousal and desire won't follow. He can be doing amazing sexual moves, but if she's writing a grocery list in her head, she won't be into it.

7. Arousal usually starts in the mind, not the body.

Arousal usually looks like this: he does something to her, and because she's paying attention, and because she's looking forward to this, her body follows. When her mind isn't engaged, arousal during sex is often much more difficult.

But *usually* and *often* are the key words here. Arousal does not *always* start in the mind. Even rape victims have been known to orgasm, and some posit that it's because the heightened state of fear can cause women's bodies to react more than usual to stimulation. Just because someone is physically aroused does not mean they consented. This phenomenon is known as arousal nonconcordance—when subjective experience is different from physical experience. For many women, our minds want to be aroused, but our bodies don't follow. For others, our minds *don't* want to be aroused, but our bodies take over.

8. The ability to "access" your arousal mechanisms is highly linked to sexual confidence.

Because arousal is closely linked to getting our brains engaged in the process, our attitudes toward sex and our sexual confidence are highly linked to our ability to attain arousal. When we feel ashamed of our bodies or ashamed of sex, or when we feel like sex is only for the guy, we're less likely to be able to feel aroused. A woman who is sexually confident can often feel "turned on" by life—she goes through her day confident of herself and who God made her, delighting in what's around her. And when she directs her attention to her sexuality rather than her surroundings, arousal is often not far behind. But when sex becomes an obligation or seems like something distasteful, then the only mechanism she has for arousal is from stimulation, which doesn't always work.

9. A woman can be aroused without being "wet."

Women can feel cognitively aroused (she's enjoying herself and wants sex!) and can even have some engorgement but not feel overly wet. Some women don't naturally produce as much lubrication as others. The amount of lubrication can also vary depending on the time of the month; it's often much heavier right before ovulation and a little lighter right afterward.

If she finds that she's not able to get lubricated, even when she subjectively feels "turned on," just pick up some lubricant! It doesn't cost much, and it can make a world of difference.

10. When menopause hits, a woman can mentally feel aroused while her body doesn't necessarily do what it once did.

Because of changes in hormone levels, after menopause a woman's body often has more difficulty with lubrication. Blood flow to the genitals is reduced, and changes in the vaginal wall can make engorgement more difficult. That doesn't mean she can't enjoy sex—it only means she may need more lubrication and more stimulation first! Use it as an excuse to draw things out and take things more slowly.

APPRECIATE HIS BODY

Women are under tremendous pressure to be beautiful. And men aren't immune either. In the last ten years, the popularity of men's beauty products and routines has exploded, including waxing and "manscaping." And all the fitness crazes and the pressure to have six-pack abs can leave guys feeling inadequate too.

Today we're going to put these doubts to rest by helping her enjoy exploring his body and helping him feel wanted.

But first one thought about how attraction differs for men and women. While what many men find sexy tends to revolve around her body, for women, that isn't always so. I remember my daughter Katie telling me that the sexiest thing about her husband, David, who has a six-pack, was when they were dating and she saw him playing with a friend's two-year-old son. Seeing him around children made her melt.

In Song of Songs, many of the traits that the woman finds attractive about the man aren't physical attributes. They're his voice, his strength, his prestige. Don't be surprised, then, if the things your wife finds sexiest aren't necessarily physical attributes—though those traits will lure her to enjoy you physically anyway!

A Note to Wives

Maybe his body has changed. He made your knees wobbly when you married him, but the years have taken their toll, and now it's hard to look at him and say hubba-hubba! He senses this. He's worried about it too.

Certainly women are held to a ridiculous standard of beauty, but increasingly, men are too. We watch movies like the Bourne series, where a great-looking guy with major muscles can take out any bad guy with a simple chop to the neck. Our guy, on the other hand, is sitting beside us on the couch, watching the movie while balancing a bowl of chips on his stomach.

Look, ladies, if we're going to complain about how women always feel like we have to live up to a crazy ideal, then let's not ask the same of our men! Maybe your husband is a little heavier now, and he isn't in the same shape as he was when you walked down the aisle. But over time you've also shared memories, intimacies, and confidences. You've built a life together. And sex is more than physical; it also unites us emotionally and spiritually. Let's concentrate on that amazing connection, and maybe the fact that he's gained some weight, lost some muscle, or is struggling with that bald spot won't matter so much.

Remember, too, that even in marriages where the husband keeps a rock-solid body, that early infatuation feeling does fade. We won't always feel weak-kneed when we look at our husbands. What becomes attractive and sexy doesn't need to be six-pack abs; it could simply be that you know he loves you and protects you and that he spends time figuring out how to make you feel good. A lover who is interested in making you feel pleasure is much better than one who may look awesome but who doesn't learn how your body works.

So spend some time tracing his body, but encourage him to trace yours too. Let him figure out how you work. If he can learn to play you like a violin, then a three-pack with a receding hairline is all you need!

A Note to Husbands

What makes a man a good lover is how he treats his wife in bed, not what his ab muscles look like. So set that as your goal! If you're on the heavier side, make sure that you hold your weight on your forearms if you're on top, or encourage her to be on top. And when you make love, use lots of foreplay and get to know her body really well. Show her affection, and take time giving her pleasure. That's what will boost her libido!

Great Sex Challenge 6

Today you're going to celebrate his greatest traits—and appreciate his body. Men, think of five attributes about yourself that you're most proud of—with at least three of them being physical traits. Wives, make a list of five things you find most attractive about your husband, with at least three physical ones. (It's okay if some are not physical. I find my husband's job kinda sexy, for instance, and I find his voice sexy.)

Once you've decided on the traits, share them with each other. Women: Affirm the ones your husband mentions. Then show him how you feel about his body! Set the timer for fifteen minutes and explore. Touch, lick, whatever you'd like to do. Get familiar with his body. Now, men: Try to hold off your orgasm. Let her explore and discover how you like to be touched. It is empowering for you to see what she likes and for her to feel sexually powerful. Give her that opportunity!

ACCOMMODATING LIBIDO DIFFERENCES

I have never met a couple without libido differences.

Almost every couple has one person who wants sex more than the other. And it's not always the guy with the higher libido either! In my survey, 24 percent of women reported having the higher libido in their marriage.

Libido differences can lead to sexual frustration, especially for the one with the higher libido. But what I really want to talk about today is the bigger problem that libido differences often reveal: both of you feel unloved.

The one with the higher libido thinks, "Why doesn't she want me?" "Does she not love me?" "Why doesn't he want to connect with me?" "Does he not want to be with me?" Because sex is so much more than physical, when someone desires sex, they're actually desiring more than that. They want real intimacy. When their spouse isn't interested in sex, it can feel like the spouse isn't interested in oneness. It's not that the spouse is rejecting sex; it's that the spouse is rejecting *them*.

Lower-libido spouses may not experience intimacy during sex in the same way (some may, for sure, but sometimes they don't). Most still want to experience intimacy, but sex isn't their primary vehicle toward oneness. Affection, physical touch, spending time together, pursuing God together, or something else they value may be what helps them feel connected and safe. When a higher-libido spouse wants sex before any of those other things, the lower-libido spouse can end up thinking, "He doesn't really love me; he only loves me for what I can do for him." Or "She's always bugging me about sex, but she doesn't really care about the things that actually matter."

Compounding this problem is the fact that we often see sex as something debased, while we may view affection as being on a higher plane. We tend to think real love is about sacrifice and service, not about a roll in the hay. This isn't a proper view of sex (as we'll see when we start our week on spiritual intimacy), but because sex is often seen as "dirty," the association remains.

All of this tends to result in a marriage where two people love each other but don't feel loved, even when there's nothing particularly wrong with the marriage. Let's see how we can navigate this minefield!

Before you do the challenge today, let's go over a few important things that need to be addressed. I'm using the terms *higher libido* and *lower libido* rather than "high" and "low" because what matters most is the *difference* in libido, not the actual libido itself. Just because someone has a lower libido does not necessarily mean they have a low libido. And just because someone has a higher libido does not mean they have a high libido. Libido isn't even static! Someone going through final exams at law school may normally have quite a high libido but may end up with a lower libido during those few months. Stress affects libido, as do physical health, mental health, emotional health, relational health, fitness level, exhaustion, medication, grief, and more. If your libido is low because of a readily discernible cause that could be fixed, such as low testosterone, I'd encourage you to see a physician. If your level of physical fitness is the issue, then improving your health can also increase your libido.

And, as we talked about previously, if the issue is a relationship problem where trust has not totally been rebuilt, then time accompanied by trustworthy behavior may improve libido as well.

Indeed, over time, as some of these issues are addressed, couples may find that their libidos flip! If libido is a struggle for you and you never want sex, I encourage you to keep up with these challenges this month with an open mind, and see if you can experience some breakthroughs.

Great Sex Challenge 7

Today's challenge comes in three parts.

1. Reassure Each Other

First, lower-libido spouses: Please understand that your spouse does love you. Indeed, the reason they want to make love so often is *because* they love you. Now, higher-libido spouses: Please understand that your spouse loves you too. Your spouse's rejection of sex is not a rejection of you as much as it is a preference for another way to connect.

One at a time, take your spouse's hand, look your spouse straight in the eyes, and reassure them of your love and your desire for intimacy.

2. Show Love

If the biggest relational problem from libido differences is this feeling of being unloved, let's figure out how to make sure each of you feels loved. Both of you take a piece of paper and a pen, and write down five things your spouse can do for you that help you feel cherished and valued. (It's okay if sex is one of those five; just make sure you include four more!) Try to choose things that are relatively easy to do and don't take much time or money—things like "bringing me a cup of coffee in the morning while I'm getting ready" or "holding my hand while we watch a movie" or "texting me during the day that you're thinking of me." Now exchange lists, and commit to trying to do several of these things a week. You'll find that if you each are regularly feeling cherished and loved, then desiring sex will often feel more natural for the lower-libido spouse.

3. SHOW DESIRE

We're going to do a repeat of one of the challenges of the last two days! This one is for the lower-libido spouse: show your spouse that you find them desirable. Today is not about exploring your spouse's body for your sake as much as it is about arousing your spouse. Show your spouse that you do enjoy their body. While in the previous two days the purpose was to enjoy exploring your spouse's body, today the purpose is simply to bring pleasure. In fact, aiming for an orgasm is absolutely okay!

One more note for the women who are the ones with lower libidos: The added benefit to this challenge is that you can feel powerful. Sometimes we women become passive in bed, letting him make most of the moves. Then we don't see what effect we can have on our guys! Take that fifteen minutes and watch how you can reduce him to a whimpering mess as he begs you for some release. That's power, girls. That's how much he wants *you*.

At the end of those fifteen minutes, do whatever you both would like. But take the full time to just touch him, because men are often so worried about whether their wives feel pleasure that to have a sexual interlude dedicated simply to making him feel good takes the pressure off and puts him on cloud nine.

Pep Talk #1

The last few days have been big challenges (don't worry; the next few days aren't quite as intense). Some of you, invariably, may have had difficulty with them. When I ran this series on my blog, one woman left this comment after the challenge about exploring her husband's body: "This one seems impossible for me. I have a history of abuse—guys forcing me to touch them—and so I have this aversion to touching my husband sexually. I enjoy sex, but I don't do much touching during it. Will I ever get through this?"

Other women emailed me saying that they found it scary to ask their husbands to touch them for fifteen minutes. It meant being so vulnerable.

But then there were others who experienced breakthroughs, like this woman:

> The kissing thing has been a big issue in our lives because my hubby had a lot of problems with his teeth so we just did not do it. So when he got his teeth worked on, we just were not doing it anymore. I always missed it, but anytime I brought it up, we ended up fighting. So I was a little nervous when the blog about kissing came up. But we did it and last night we kissed like we haven't kissed in years. I am about to start crying while I type this. It was so wonderful, and I feel closer to my husband today than I have in forever. It just opened something up in me. And as a side note, it did lead to the first big O I have had in about 6 months.
>
> Thank you and can't wait to see what is in store for the rest of the month.

Some of you working through these 31 days are just looking for a tune-up, or a way to turn the knob from 9 to a 10. That's wonderful! **If that's you—feel free to proceed straight to day 8.**

But a lot of you have some major issues when it comes to sex, either because you've brought baggage into your marriage or because marriage has given you baggage. Sex is the one area you fight about a lot, and it has just never clicked. And you find yourself really worried about whether it can get better.

That's why today I want to give you a chance to pause to get some perspective, relax, and take stock.

I firmly believe that with most things in life, what matters is not so much where we are but the direction we are going. If you have enjoyed a great sex life in the past, but right now you barely talk to each other and you're super busy, you're probably in worse shape than a woman who has never experienced an orgasm but who is enthusiastic about connecting with her husband and trying to work through any issues. In the long run, the person with the right attitude and goals will come out better than the person who started off well but isn't putting in the effort to maintain what they had.

The purpose during these 31 days is not to compare yourself with anyone else, and it's not to force yourself to achieve something. It's simply to start moving in the right direction. This is the fork in the road, and you've decided to walk along the road that will bring you closer to real intimacy on all levels. That doesn't mean you're going to arrive—nor do you have to! But at least you're moving in the right direction.

Here, then, are some things to remember to make this 31-day challenge work for you.

DON'T BE GOAL-ORIENTED. BE DIRECTION-ORIENTED.

You want to feel more relaxed, more confident, and more positive about sex—but you don't need to feel *completely* relaxed, *completely* confident, or *completely* positive about sex. Don't pressure yourself. Just commit to keeping an open mind, a positive attitude, and an "I'll try anything once" spirit!

ADAPT TO FIT YOUR CIRCUMSTANCES

After day 6 I told the woman who had emailed about being abused in the past to change the challenge so that instead of sexually stimulating her husband, she just got used to enjoying feeling him naked—even if all she did was give him a massage. You know yourself best; if you have to adapt, adapt.

But do try to do the challenges because the way I've set them up, they're not usually intimidating. I'm not trying to get you to do a particular thing; I'm trying to urge you to explore. With the day 6 challenge, for instance, she was the one in control, which is often much less scary for women with baggage. If she is in control and sets the parameters, it's sometimes easier for her to enjoy herself!

BE PATIENT WITH YOUR SPOUSE

If your spouse isn't embracing the challenges as much as you'd like or is acting nervous, be patient. You can't force intimacy. Many of us have baggage holding us back. Gentleness is the best way to deal with it. Exasperation or impatience often drives people further away.

If your spouse is struggling, reassure them of your love and acceptance and dedication to making sure you *both* feel intimacy in your marriage. You can start by showing patience now. Tell your spouse that you can take your time and ease into it.

And remember: marriage is a lifetime commitment! You have time to get this right.

Now, if you're ready to go on to another challenge tonight, by all means start day 8. But if you've been struggling, it may be a better idea to redo one of the previous ones or just spend the night snuggling before you move on to the next challenge. It's okay to go back and do day 5 again—or even day 6—until you feel more comfortable, less anxious, and ready to move ahead.

Heads up: the next challenge includes some ideas that you do during the day or before heading to bed, so it may be best to read it together in the morning.

DAYS 8–11

Laughter

(Emotional Intimacy)

14 WAYS TO PLAY AS A COUPLE

When my older daughter was eight, she asked what I wanted for Christmas. When I didn't mention any toys, she felt sorry for me. "Why don't you like to play anymore, Mommy?"

Why do we stop playing? Maybe Polly Pocket and Barbie aren't your cup of tea, but laughing and giggling and joking should be—because it's good for your marriage and for your soul!

So far we've looked at some of the roadblocks to enjoying a good sex life, and for many of you, this has brought up issues of low self-esteem, sexual baggage from the past, and more. That's awfully heavy. Today, before we get to more "sexual" challenges, I want to address something at the root of many of our marriage problems: we stop having fun together. And when we stop having fun, marriage becomes so, well, *serious*.

Addressing problems in our marriages—whether they're related to sex, parenting, finances, time, or whatever—is ever so much easier if we also find time to laugh together. A couple who laughs together is also a couple who enjoys being together and will find navigating all the difficulties of marriage much easier.

Today I want to present you with a list of fourteen ways to play together as a couple. These aren't necessarily sexual—although you can certainly put a sexual spin on them if you want to. Later in the week we'll look at how to flirt together, but today I want to focus on laughter—laughter inspired by physical fun. When we have "physical" fun together, sexual fun often follows.

Before you launch into these "play" ideas, set the mood. If you want to have fun with your spouse, make sure they are in the right frame of mind and know something playful is coming. Don't just spring something on your spouse when they're worried about work or are preoccupied. Send texts throughout the day, kiss lots when you're home, and laugh a lot beforehand. Then go for it.

1. **Have a water fight.** When you do the dishes, flick some water on your spouse, and see what happens! Or, to turn it up a notch, give each other water guns, and go for it! (May work better when it's not winter, for those of us in the Great White North.)

2. **Throw a snowball.** If snow is plentiful, text your spouse to warn them to be on their guard tonight. Then set up an ambush! You can ask the kids to join in the fun too. Physical play doesn't have to exclude the kids, and all of you laughing together and ending up breathless is still a great preview of what could happen later that night.

3. **Wrestle.** I often win wrestling matches because we make a deal. I have to move my husband (if he's standing) or push him off the bed (if he's lying down). He's not allowed to use anything to stop me, except his body and perhaps two fingers. I can do anything I want. And even with those concessions, I still can't move him! But he laughs so hard that he often loses. But sometimes I let him win quickly because what hubby doesn't like to get his wife right where he wants her? We always have fun wrestling, and it almost always leads to other things.

4. **Have a pillow fight!** Ambush your spouse with a pillow. Then run while they try to get you back!

5. **Throw a "pie in the face."** Eating chocolate cake tonight? Or making pudding? Smear it on him—and be prepared for it to be returned.

6. **Act out a scene from a movie.** My friend J from the blog *Hot, Holy & Humorous* recommends acting out dancing scenes or romantic scenes from movies. She says, "Turn off the sound, and have the two of you provide the audio. See what fun or sexy lines you can come up with!" Or take the approach that Steve Carell and Tina Fey did in *Date Night*: when you're out in public, watch a couple talking, and make up dialogue for them or describe a funny scenario of what they're doing together. Just laugh!

7. **Dance.** Turn your kitchen floor or your living room floor into a dance floor! Turn up the music, and dip and swing to your heart's content! Even if you don't know what you're doing, moving together can lead to lots of laughs.

8. **Box.** If you own an interactive gaming system, try a boxing game! You'll raise your heart rate, and she may just be able to knock him out!

9. **Hit the courts.** Play squash, badminton, tennis, or another racquet sport. Make whoever is better play with their nondominant hand.

10. **Play slapjack to the death.** Each of you take half the deck of cards and keep flipping them up, one by one. Whenever one of you flips up a jack, you slap the cards! Whoever slaps first gets the deck. Winner is the one left holding the cards. It's super quick, and you'll be slapping down those cards so hard that you'll work up a sweat! Winner gets something of their choice—could be something sexual or something like getting out of doing the dishes or taking a bath while the loser puts the kids to bed.

11. **Play indoor volleyball.** Blow up some balloons and play volleyball over the bed—in the nude!

12. **Have a tickling contest.** Who will cry uncle first?

13. **Turn chores into a game.** One of my Facebook followers gave me this idea:

> When we change the sheets on the bed, we have a race to see who can finish putting the pillowcase on the pillow and get the pillow on the bed in its place first. We do things like hide

the opponent's pillowcase, throw pillows downstairs, grab opponent's pillow, yank the pillowcase off and toss it in the hall, lock each other in the bathroom, and wrestle each other for our own pillowcase that the other is hoarding, hiding, or trying to throw out the window. Much laughter, much tickling, much running through the house and acting like children. It's fun!

14. **Food fight.** Finally, there's the staple from the high school cafeteria: a food fight. If you're cooking with your hubby and "accidentally" get flour on his nose, what will he do back? There's something about play-fighting that often ends in an embrace, and isn't that most of the fun?

Great Sex Challenge 8

Today's challenge is simple: play! Pick an item—and do it!

Heads up: the next challenge includes some other ideas that you do throughout the day, so it may be best to read it together in the morning—or read it tomorrow night, assuming you'll do it the next day.

Day 9

Preparing for Sex throughout the Day

I hope you all had fun playing yesterday! Try to incorporate play into your marriage; it makes intimacy more natural. Now we've got ourselves thinking in the right direction and laughing together to smooth over issues and increase goodwill. But what about getting in a frisky frame of mind?

For many men that's not much of a challenge. You just start thinking about sex, and you're ready to go!

But for many women, the mere thought of sex isn't enough to rev our engines, especially if other things are on our minds. That's why it's important to lay the groundwork so that when you are together, sex seems like an attractive proposition.

Today I'm going to talk mostly to the wives, though at the end I will have some special words of wisdom for the guys. But if you are a guy with a lower libido than your wife, I recommend going through some of the following information and applying what you can (and excuse me for using feminine pronouns—just switch them in your head).

Getting in the right frame of mind doesn't mean you have to be actively thinking about sex throughout the day. No one wants to be

71

trying to get excited while talking to the boss or while taking toddlers out for a walk.

But there's more to being sexual than just thinking or fantasizing. There's also feeling comfortable in your own skin, feeling comfortable with your spouse, and getting rid of roadblocks to enjoying sex tonight. Here's a game plan to help you use your day well:

Prepare Your Body

I live in the Great White North, where there are two seasons: winter and construction. And winter is substantially longer, so many northern gals throw those razors away in the winter. What's the point of shaving when no one can see your legs?

No one, that is, except you and your husband. And let's face it: how sexy are you going to feel with "man legs"? Honestly, it doesn't take that long to shave (if you do shave; if you don't, that's okay). But if you shave in the summer and feel good about it, then stop in the winter, how sexy do you think you'll feel when you're nude in the middle of January? There's something about shaving that can make us feel pretty and prepared.

Make your body itself feel great! Shave and use lots of lotion to keep your skin soft and smooth. When you feel better in your skin, you'll enjoy feeling skin on skin far more.

Prepare Your Clothes

Kiss frumpiness goodbye. Wear clothes that make you feel attractive and that flatter your shape. Don't have clothes that make you feel confident? Go buy some! Having six outfits that make you feel amazing is better than having fifty T-shirts and seven pairs of mom jeans that make you feel dowdy.

Looking and feeling attractive during the day will boost your confidence level at night. And don't forget our day 3 challenge from last week: concentrate on those five areas of your body that you're proud of. Don't focus on what you don't like about your body; *think about what you do.*

Note to the guys: You can still boost your libido by feeling more attractive and more like a man! At night try to ditch the sloppy T-shirts with those old slogans like "McGonigal's Bank Bike for Cancer," and buy some attractive pajamas. Biking for cancer is great; being reminded about it with an outdated, oversized, holey T-shirt is not sexy. When you get home from work, especially if you work an active job, head to the shower first and suds up, then brush your teeth. When you're clean, she'll be more receptive, and you'll feel more in the mood too.

Carve Out Some "Me" Time

One of the biggest impediments to female libido is exhaustion. When I took surveys of two thousand women for my *Good Girl's Guide to Great Sex*, the number one thing women reported that was wrecking their sex lives was simply being tired. When we feel like everyone is depending on us and our plates are overflowing with tasks, we're going to crave time to ourselves. And when do we take that time? When the kids are in bed—right when you could be romantic with your husband!

If you need forty-five minutes to yourself every day, find a way to build it into your routine. It is okay to stick the kids in front of a video for forty-five minutes so you can work on a hobby if you want to. Having a great marriage is more important than spending every waking minute stimulating your children. If you work outside the home, use your lunch hours to rejuvenate yourself however works best. Have lunch with coworkers if you need adult conversation, cocoon yourself in a corner with a book if you need some alone time, or head to the gym.

Make a list of activities that would help to center you and make you feel sane—whether it's doing a hobby for half an hour, reading a book, soaking in a bath, or going for a jog. Then figure out how you can make these activities a reality. If you can take that time to yourself during the day, you will be more rejuvenated at night.

If you just can't see where that time is going to come from, then talk to your hubby and explain why you need it. Maybe he'll volunteer to put the kids to bed just so you can take a bubble bath!

Note to the guys: This is just as important for you if you have a high-stress job during the day. Try to resist the urge to bring work home, or if you have to, put a time limit on it. And don't let that time limit be "I'll stop at bedtime." Stop a good two hours before you plan to turn in with your wife so that you have time to decompress. One of the leading causes of a low libido is high stress. When you're stressed, you're not as productive. Carving out time to relax is key to your productivity at work and to your intimacy in marriage.

Plan Regular Times to Imagine Sex

When men haven't had sex in a while, their bodies feel it. Most women don't experience this, so they need a reminder, or a trigger, to think sexy! What about choosing one activity, or one trigger point, that makes you smile or think about the last great encounter you had? Say, every time you do the dishes, you think about your favorite sexual memory. Or perhaps every time you're at a stop sign or every time you hear a siren. Then you can text your husband and say, "Remember when . . ."

Sleep

Getting some shut-eye may not sound exciting, but it is awfully important! If exhaustion is a big culprit in killing our libidos, then we have to treat sleep seriously. Most of us need at least eight hours of sleep. If you get up at 6:30 a.m., then you need to get to sleep at 10:30 p.m. That's *getting to sleep*—not crawling into bed and turning on the TV in your bedroom or scrolling through Facebook or even having sex. It means lights out—which also means you should be crawling into bed closer to 9:45 if you want time to cuddle, talk, and have fun with your spouse.

Note to the guys: Don't watch TV in your bedroom too late and keep her awake. And don't watch TV or play video games until midnight and then hope she's still energetic. If your work and childcare schedule allow, think about making love as an early evening activity (or a morning activity if necessary!). Work together to help her get rid of some roadblocks to making love, and you'll find you both feel more confident and more intimate.

Great Sex Challenge 9

Your mission, should you choose to accept it, is to help both of you have an easier time getting in a frisky frame of mind. Go through the suggestions above and decide what one or two concrete steps you can take, either individually or as a couple, to work toward that goal. If all the points apply to you, pick the ones that resonate most. It's easier to make changes that stick if you try to change a few things rather than trying to change everything at once. Then rejoice about your new game plan!

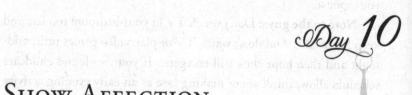

Day 10

SHOW AFFECTION

Remember our fifteen-second kiss a day? I hope you're still smooching away! It's so important to help us feel connected.

We've talked about how to play together and how to think about and prepare for sex throughout the day. Tomorrow we're going to turn to how to flirt! But before we get there, let's talk about affection.

For some of us, sex is the need and affection is the choice. For others, affection feels more like the need and sex feels more like the choice.

Ponder those statements for a moment. Whichever one is your biggest need, likely your spouse feels the need for the other with pretty much the same intensity.

In our culture, affection has largely been separated from sex. Sex is no longer about a connection between two people as much as it is about a quest for an orgasm (not that there's anything wrong with orgasms!). But sex becomes about the body and not about the soul or the relationship or even about love. And for women, especially, that's a stretch. If sex in your marriage has become something that is tacked on at the end of a day when you didn't touch, didn't say sweet words to each other, and didn't laugh together, it can easily feel as if you are simply using each other. For her, especially, that can be very difficult.

Affection conveys the message *I cherish you*. Sex, then, is not only about the joining of two bodies but about the joining of two hearts.

Here are some ideas for how to be affectionate with each other.

Take a Hand

Whenever you're walking with each other or sitting beside each other, hold hands.

Touch

As you walk past each other, make it a habit to reach out and brush a shoulder or pat an arm or ruffle some hair. Especially if your spouse's love language is touch, it's important to reach out and make that quick connection—a connection that isn't overtly sexual!

Say Kind Things

When my husband and I speak at marriage conferences, my husband tells the story of a couple who had been married for forty-five years. One day, in desperation, the wife announced that they needed counseling. He was flabbergasted. "Why?" he asked. She replied, "You never talk to me. You never touch me. I don't even think you love me anymore." He rolled his eyes and replied, "Look, on our wedding day I told you that I loved you. If that ever changes, I'll let you know."

Don't be like that guy. Make it a habit, every day, to tell your wife you love her.

And women, make it a habit, every day, to tell your husband *why* you love him. Don't just say I love you. Say, "I appreciate so much how you provide for the family," or "The way you play with Jeffy makes me so happy. He loves you so much," or "The way you handled that disagreement at church made me so proud to be your wife." Note what he does well, and tell him those things.

That's it. Just hold hands, touch, and say kind things. It's amazing how those three little actions can change the whole atmosphere of a marriage!

Great Sex Challenge 10

Hold hands while you talk through tonight's challenge!

Answer this question: What one kind of nonsexual affection do you crave most?

Now share with each other two or three things that most attracted you to your spouse when you met. What did you love about him? What did you love about her? Tell each other—in great detail!

10 Ways Husbands Can Help Wives Get in the Mood

For Marriages Where She Has the Lower Libido

Unlike most men, women, on the whole, aren't usually "raring to go." We need to warm up to the idea of sex. That may seem odd because most women do enjoy sex, so why wouldn't we want to do it all the time? But if we're not specifically thinking about it and in the mood, then the idea of sex seems almost off-putting. A switch needs to be flipped so that we move from "turned off" to "turned on." For most (though not all) guys, that switch is almost always on; for women, it's not. Here's the hard thing about that switch: *guys can't flip it for us.* We need to turn it on ourselves.

We need to decide: "Okay, I want to feel sexy now."

A husband's job is simply to warm up a woman so that she is more likely to want to flip that switch. If he acts as if the switch is already flipped by making obvious sexual comments or by grabbing parts of her body as she walks by, chances are that she won't react well. But warm her up first so that she flips that switch, and then those advances are absolutely okay!

One woman explained this brilliantly on my Facebook page: "Don't act sexy! After a long day I don't want to feel propositioned. I want to feel like he's my best friend, like he still enjoys my conversation—laughing with me, etc. I want to know he thinks about and considers me!"

Here's the general progression:

Warming up → Flirty → Sexual

Once a wife is obviously flirting, then ramping it up is fine. But if she's still at the warming up stage, don't go straight to the sexual!

So, without further ado, here are ten "sexy" questions that will help women feel flirty and in the mood!

1. What can I do to help?

Women overwhelmingly report that the sexiest thing a man can say is, "Can I do the dishes tonight?" or "Can I do the kids' bedtime routine on my own tonight?" or "What can I do to make your evening run more smoothly?" When I asked on Facebook for ideas for how husbands can get wives in the mood, over half of all responses were some variation of this.

So take the hint! One reason that women have a hard time getting in the mood is that nighttime is busy and chaotic, and so much is running through our brains. Take some of that load off, and we'll be able to calm down a bit and have some quiet, peaceful moments. That can lead to more energetic moments!

2. How was your day?

When women know their husbands care about their hearts, they often can jump from zero to sixty in no time. In a similar vein, try

"How are you feeling?" Not just "Are you okay?" but "How are you feeling?"

Sometimes women get so lost in their heads that they need a place to put all those feelings to make room for sexy thoughts. It often doesn't take long to make room!

3. Did you get more beautiful today?

One woman reported, "Yesterday my husband just looked me deep in the eyes out of the blue like he was surprised and said, 'Did you get more beautiful today?' Caught me totally off-guard. Probably wouldn't work every day, but it was really sweet!"

Another woman said a similar thing: "In the shower the other day, my hubby randomly said, 'Gosh, you are pretty. Do you know that?' That made me get butterflies!"

We want to know we can still take your breath away! And guys, if you're going to compliment her looks (which you should), don't mention the traditional "sexy" parts right off the bat. Sweet works better than sexy when you're just warming up!

4. May I massage your feet?

Pretty much every woman who follows me on Facebook agreed that offering a massage is always a good choice. A massage feels wonderful, but it also allows some physical contact that helps her feel more "in the mood," and it relaxes her so she's able to get all those distractions out of her head that can keep her from wanting to make love.

Here's a similar one: "Do you want to cuddle?" Anything that suggests touching and physical contact that isn't overtly sexual tends to go over well. It lets us know we're enjoyed simply for being us, and not for just our bodies.

5. How did I get so blessed to marry a woman who is such a wonderful mom? (Or insert other great character trait here!)

A woman explains: "A character compliment ('I'm proud of you,' or 'Our kids are so lucky to have you for a mom') is a huge turn-on. I know he's attracted to me, but hearing that he sees what I do and believes in me as a person is more sexy than almost anything else."

Please hear her, guys, because this is important: we know you want our bodies. We want to know you want our brains and souls as well!

6. When did you know I was the one?

Ask something that brings up romantic memories!

Reliving dating and newlywed days gets many women's romance meters firing. Ask questions like: What did you think about me when we first met? When did you know I was the one? What do you remember about our first date? What are your best memories of our honeymoon?

When you're the one who asks the question, you're saying, "I want to relive this with you because it mattered to me too." Bring up those feelings, and see where they go!

7. Don't ask a question at all. Just show that you noticed something she cares about.

Paying attention to the details shows your wife you love her. You could say, "I remember hearing you say you love peanut M&M's, so I picked some up for you on the way home."

A woman explains: "Being 'seen' and 'heard' is sexy! I am so harried that having my husband make statements instead of asking a question is usually more valuable than asking a question (unless it is seeking my opinion about a flavor of chocolate/coffee). Children ask questions. Husbands make statements that show they notice: 'You've got a lot done today. I'd like to sit with you on the deck before going to bed. I started a pot of coffee.' My eyes see stars!!!"

Now, if she's all warmed up and it's time to start the flirty stage, try these sexier questions!

8. I've been thinking about you all day, and what I'd like to do.

Some women would rather get right to the point! And if you're going to get right to the point, explain to her what you want to do, because a woman's libido is often linked to feeling desired rather than to desiring something herself. So instead of saying, "I'm going to do X to you later," try "I want to do X and see Y later." It's a subtle shift, but it matters.

9. Can I get you out of those clothes? They look so uncomfortable.

Or even switch roles: "I'm so uncomfortable in these clothes. Can you help me get them off?" That's flirty and suggestive but not blatantly graphic or sexual.

10. How can I make you moan louder?

Save this one until everything is heated up and going well—and it will likely go even better. Or throw this one in too: "We tried something last time that you really liked, but I can't remember what it was. Can we experiment until we figure it out?" Show her you're interested in her pleasure and you want to learn, and she'll feel much more cherished!

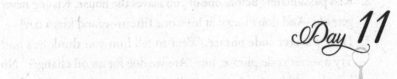

FLIRT WITH YOUR SPOUSE!

When we're dating we flirt. She winks at him. He takes her hand. She gives him that "come hither" look. But when we're married, too often we stop flirting. Why flirt when you've already got her? And if she flirts, she may worry that she'll give him the impression that she's definitely going to deliver tonight. You wouldn't want to promise that when you have no idea how you'll feel later!

But there's a problem with that strategy. A woman's primary sex organ is her brain. For us to get in the mood, our brains have to be engaged. Take flirting out of the equation, and you take away one of our primary tools for boosting our libidos! And feeling desired by our spouses is another big libido boost, as long as it's done in the right way.

We're one-third of the way through our *31 Days to Great Sex*, and two days ago we looked at how to prepare your mind for sex throughout the day. We weren't looking at anything particularly frisky, just things to make you feel more at ease, more confident, and less tired.

Today we're going to turn it up a notch by learning to flirt! Just as playing together helps you laugh together, flirting helps you laugh—and binds you together because you share a relationship with your spouse that is truly unique. Here are some ideas to get the fun rolling.

1. **Leave a love note on the mirror.** Using a dry erase marker (or even lipstick!), leave a love note on your honey's bathroom mirror. To be even bolder, draw a picture of what you want to do later.

2. **Kiss passionately before one of you leaves the house.** Kissing never gets old. And don't forget at least one fifteen-second kiss a day!

3. **Have a secret code phrase.** Want to tell him you think he's hot? Try a secret code phrase, like "Are we due for an oil change?" No one else will know what you really mean, so you can say it in front of the kids, in front of your parents, in front of anybody!

4. **Play the fortune cookie game.** Whenever you get a fortune cookie, mentally add the words *in bed* to the end of the message. You'll giggle together at a Chinese restaurant as you pass it to your husband, but your kids will never know why you're laughing!

5. **Grab some flesh.** When he's walking by, smack his butt! Now, here's where the situation may differ for the guys. If she's doing the dishes and you walk up behind her and squeeze her breasts, she's likely to get a little ticked off. Many women write to me saying, "My husband is always grabbing me! It makes me feel so used!" Men may not mean it that way, and many men enjoy being grabbed. But women don't in the same way.

   While women can be bolder, then, it's often better for men to start off with a lighter touch. Instead of grabbing her breast, stroke her shoulder. If you're sitting on the couch next to her, run your fingers through her hair. Hold her hand as often as you can. If she giggles and returns the attention, then by all means, try something a little friskier!

6. **Set up a cozy love nest for watching movies.** Want to watch a flick tonight? Share pillows and a blanket and play footsie. One respondent to my survey for *The Good Girl's Guide to Great Sex* said that she and her husband have "topless movies," where they snuggle up under the blankets minus their tops. Tons of fun!

7. **Wives, ask your husband to choose your panties for the day.** If he chooses them, he'll be picturing you in nothing but them.

8. **Text, text, text each other.** Text about anything—song lyrics, memories of fun times you've had, what you're wearing, what you're thinking about. "Looking forward to seeing all of you tonight . . ."

9. **Stick notes in your spouse's lunch.** One of my Facebook fans shared this idea: "I also write stuff on his brown bag lunch. For a while, I thought it might embarrass him. But when I stopped, he pouted. They aren't always 'sexy.' Some are just sweet. But tomorrow's lunch has written in red letters: 'For my Red-Hot Lover!'"

10. **Flash him—but not in public.** If he's goofing off on his computer or playing a video game or relaxing on the couch, walk by and open up your robe to reveal nothing at all. Then keep walking, and see what he does!

    A commenter on my blog also recommended doing chores vigorously—and bralessly—so he can appreciate the bounce! When you mop the floor, wear a skirt but go commando and get down on all fours to see if he notices.

11. **Drop something "by accident."** It's okay to make this one a little bit silly. Stand right in front of him, and then—*whoops!*—you dropped your pen. (Remember the movie *Legally Blonde*? Bend— and *snap!*) Or your earring. Make a big production of bending over right in front of him and trying to find it on the floor.

12. **Stick a surprise somewhere interesting.** Another reader emailed me this tidbit:

My husband recently got back from a long out-of-state trip. It was late when he got home but I was expecting him. He quickly showered and came to our room in new underwear (that was a color! something I had been longing for). He said, "I have something for you." I thought it was the underwear and I commented on how nice they were between smooching. "No, I have a gift for you in them." I thought he was just being cheeky—of course he is a gift! So I reached on in and there was a jewelry box!!!! That was not what I expected! It was a sweet gift, and his creativity was so memorable! He has inspired my own games of hide and seek, may it be a note written with a wash-off marker under my panty line or some little item in my bra . . . it is a fun way to play every now and then.

13. **Get messy.** Doing dishes? Blow some bubbles her way. Washing the car? Spray him a little bit, especially in an interesting place. Show your spouse, "I want to play with you!"

14. **Eat enthusiastically.** If you're eating your favorite food, like chocolate cake or apple pie, make a production out of it. Moan a lot over how much you're enjoying it. Act like you're in raptures. He'll recognize that sound and want to take it further!

15. **Play "strip" anything.** Turn any board game into a sexy time by adding "strip" to the beginning: Strip Battleship (an item of clothing for each ship sunk), Strip Scrabble (for every word worth twenty to thirty points), Strip Monopoly (every time you pass go or an item of clothing to get out of jail), etc.

16. **Play footsie.** When you're at a restaurant with tablecloths, slip your shoe off, and let your toes explore your spouse's legs. Give your spouse a preview of what's ahead, while you just carry on a normal conversation!

Flirting Rules of Engagement for Her

A few ground rules. When you flirt, you're telling your husband, *I'm interested. I find you attractive. I want you.* If you add flirting into your relationship, you're going to have to make sure you add some sex in there too, or else your guy is going to get mixed messages (and he'll be very frustrated).

Does flirting mean you have to follow through each and every time? No, not at all. But allow me to give you a bit of insight into how husbands often work. Most men don't just want sex because it physically feels good. They want to feel wanted. Flirting is one of those ways they feel wanted. If it's followed up by regular and frequent sex, most guys won't mind if you don't have sex for a night or two, even if you did flirt. When men get regular and frequent sex, they become much more secure and confident that we love them.

One of the reasons men often seem desperate for sex is because they're desperate to know they're desired. It's not only the physical release they need: it's that emotional and even spiritual validation that says, *I value and want you.* When they're getting that from you regularly, then you have a lot more room to play and kiss and flirt without necessarily having to make love right then and there. When you're not making love with your husband frequently and regularly, though, he'll be much less able to flirt without being frustrated if nothing happens.

So if you're thinking, "Every time I kiss my husband, he wants it to go somewhere," or "Every time I flirt, he wants something else," that may be because your husband is insecure about whether you really want him, because sex is infrequent, or perhaps because you never initiate.

This month we're going to talk more about how to get you more in the mood and how to make it more fun and less stressful for you so that you desire sex more often. But for right now, here's the message: flirting is a fun way to play with your husband, to boost your own libido, to get you thinking along those lines, and to make your husband feel wanted. And if it's combined with regular sex, you'll feel much more confident in your relationship if you throw in some of these fun ideas!

What if you flirt, though, and your husband doesn't take the hint? You put on something sexy, but he doesn't look up from the TV? Or he finds sexy talk a bother because he has too much on his mind? That's when you may have to get more margin in your life as a couple so that his mind is not taken up only with time wasters or with work. Spend some time together in the evenings without screens and without work. We'll be talking about putting that into practice in later challenges.

Flirting Rules of Engagement for Him

Flirting is a ton of fun, but instead of thinking of flirting as saying to her, "Let's have sex!" think of flirting as a way to communicate to her, "I love you. I value you. I think you're a ton of fun." Think of it as something that will make you giggle together rather than as a prelude to something else. It's an extension of the affection exercise we did yesterday, only turned up a notch.

I know that can be a tall order, but many women feel objectified: *he only wants me for one thing.* That can make flirting the last thing they want to do. Removing flirting from a marriage entirely, though, also removes a lot of the fun! So add affection, add lots of touch, and add lots of giggles. Then take your cues from her. If she gets racier, feel free to go for it!

And a note to the guys who aren't responding to flirting: If your wife is trying to get you in the mood and trying to get you laughing, but you're too distracted with work or other things and find it bothersome, then please, carve out some time when you do respond to your wife. And if she flirts but it's not a good time, say, "I'd love to, honey, but can you give me twenty more minutes to finish what I've started?" Put a timeline on it, and then honor that timeline. Women need to feel wanted, and if you rebuff her attempts at flirting, you'll add a layer of rejection and hurt to your marriage.

Great Sex Challenge 11

Sprinkle these ideas into your next few days until they become natural. And think of some of your own! Throw yourself into them. Have fun with them. Get in a truly flirty frame of mind, and you may find that your own libido goes up because the fun quotient in your marriage goes up.

10 Sexy Questions to Ask Your Husband

For Men with the Higher Libido— or Who Appreciate Initiation!

Ladies, if he's got the higher libido and you want to do more than flirt, here are ten questions that will rev his engines and make him feel pursued.

1. Guess what panties I'm wearing!

This one's fun to ask on the phone too!

2. What's the last sexy dream you had?

Be ready to reply with one of your own. He'll likely turn the tables on you!

3. If you could relive any of our sexual moments, which ones would you choose?

Find out what he's enjoyed the most—and then repeat it.

4. At our wedding reception, what were you thinking of doing to me?

Ask him what he anticipated most. If he's not specific, then ask some follow-up questions. "Were you looking forward more to X or Y? What part of my body drove you the craziest, Y or Z?" Find out how desperately he wanted to leave the party!

5. When we're making love, what position gives you your favorite view?

Then ask him why!

Now let's turn it up a notch.

6. Is this too revealing?

Put on your tightest top or your shortest skirt (that you never wear out of the house, of course!), or wear just a bra and a camisole. Walk by him and bend over and ask what he thinks. Be sure to run your hands over the part you're "worried" about.

7. Which affects you more?

Does he enjoy looking at your body? Do a little fashion show. Choose two outfits or lingerie sets, and ask him which has the greater effect on him.

Bonus points: Check it out for yourself! Feel what kind of an effect you're having on him, and see which one works better.

8. Is it better like this or like this?

Put on your best innocent voice, as in "I just want to learn and I'm honestly curious," and ask him which two parts of his body he prefers you to kiss or rub, or choose one part of his body and kiss or rub it in two ways. This one can continue as long as you want—just keep changing what you're doing. And keep the wide-eyed, innocent look going, as in "I'm just trying to learn, honey. Why would you think anything else?"

9. How fast can you go?

I like this question because it's a way of turning the tables on a night that may not necessarily go very far for you! Let's say you're a little stressed and you don't think you can enjoy sex too much tonight. Or maybe you're just hormonal and it's not a great time of the month for your libido.

If you still want to have some fun, even if it's not primarily for you, be the active one. Climb on top, or whisper to him, "How fast can you go?" Give him permission not to worry about pleasing you, and he can go wild.

10. Could you give me a hand in here?

Getting ready for work in the morning? Or having a late Saturday morning? Climb in the shower while he's in the bathroom and then ask him for some help. He'd better get the hint and jump in there with you!

Pep Talk #2

My plan for this month was to lay out a strategy to help you get the most out of your marriage. Why settle for mediocre when sex is a vital part of your relationship—one that God designed to bind you together, to give you great pleasure, and to add fun and sparks to your life?

This week is going to be one you've hopefully been anticipating: we're going to explore how to make sex feel physically stupendous. But when I published a version of this 31-day challenge on my blog, right about now I started receiving plenty of emails from people who were finding it too difficult, usually because they had a lot of sexual baggage and they just didn't want sex.

Many wrote saying that for the first time, they felt like they were connecting. But others wrote with basically no hope. How can anyone tell you sex can be good when it obviously is not?

If you're having a great time, feel free to move straight to day 12!

But others of you think this is hopeless. Please, hear me out. Don't you wish it were different? Don't you wish sex could be good? Do you want to live your life with this distance between you? Your spouse needs you to try, to believe it can get better. One way you can do this is just to try what I'm suggesting with an open mind. These ideas aren't the answer to all your problems, and if you have a better way, that's fine. But please, try *something*.

When you have children, you owe it to them to do what's in your power to make your marriage rock-solid, and that includes having a close, intimate relationship with your spouse. If sex is a huge road-block, that's okay. But can you try to imagine that it's not? Believe that it doesn't have to stay this way. Your main sex organ is your brain. What you think about sex will largely determine your arousal level, the pleasure you get from sex, and your desire for sex. So can you just try? Just take little baby steps?

If you go back to the beginning of these challenges, you'll find that's what I'm recommending: baby steps. So please don't give up. You were made for more than this. You were made to truly experience intimacy. Right now you may not see how that could happen, but can you try?

Pray about your sex life, together if you can. Pray that God will give you his mind about sex and repair some of the lies you might have believed. If you don't think you've believed lies, but you just hate sex, then pray anyway, and ask God to show you how your situation can be better and where you may be sabotaging yourself.

Please try. For yourself and for your marriage.

Days 12–19

Igniting Fireworks

(Physical Intimacy)

Getting Her Head
in the Game

We've looked at how to reframe our thoughts about sex, how we think about our bodies and about pleasure, and even how to think of our spouses differently. We've looked at how to get in the right frame of mind by flirting, playing, and preparing for sex. Now we're going to turn to what to do when the time finally arrives. Today we're going to look at how to get her head in the game, and then later this week we'll turn to foreplay, orgasm, and more!

Let me start with a basic fact that many men and women don't understand about female libido, and it goes like this: if her head isn't in the game, it's difficult for her to get aroused. Most men react to the thought of sex almost automatically; women need to decide to react—and decide to become aroused.

I've often heard it said that men are like microwaves and women are like slow cookers, insinuating that men can heat up and be done quickly, while women take more time. But I think that analogy is flawed because it implies that women will, eventually, heat up. The truth is that there is no guarantee. A guy can do to his wife exactly the same thing that yesterday had her in raptures, and today he can tell she's lying there thinking, "Will you just get it over with because

95

I want to get to sleep." While women certainly can heat up, men can't completely do it for us. We control the switch. We're the ones who need to decide to participate, and that isn't always easy.

Consider this scenario:

She walks into the bedroom to find her husband giving her that "Y'wanna?" look. She smiles and begins to undress while he looks on appreciatively. She climbs into bed and they start kissing.

Then suddenly, out of nowhere, she pushes him away and says, "Do you think Michelle should drop piano? She just isn't enjoying it and it's costing us twenty dollars a week in lessons and a whole Tuesday night. We could take that money and go to a movie as a family and spend quality time together instead!"

What just happened? Did she decide she really didn't want to have sex? Chances are that her husband was pretty disappointed and very confused because he thought the evening was going in a certain direction, and now she has erected a big detour sign.

I used to think that when I launched into a big monologue right in the middle of foreplay, I was subconsciously trying to push my husband away. But over the years I've realized the opposite is the case. I can't get into making love if I have a lot of unprocessed thoughts in my head, because they end up bouncing around in there like a huge pinball game. And my body doesn't suddenly spring into action the way my husband's does. I have to get myself in the mood, anticipate what we're doing, and concentrate if it's going to feel good. As with most women, sex for me is mostly in my head.

And if there's too much other stuff rolling around in my head, my body can't get in the game. Part of a woman's getting ready for the big event, then, is to empty her head of all the thoughts rattling around in there. When she can get those out, she can let other stuff in. For external processors, like me, that means taking time earlier in the evening to talk. For internal processors, it may mean having some alone time to think or pray or journal. But we have to get these distractions out!

Another element of a woman's readiness to jump into bed relates specifically to the urge to talk. For many men, making love is a way of checking in on the relationship and making sure that everything is good. When they make love with their wives, they feel as if their wives accept them and want to be with them.

But many women need to feel that acceptance first, and part of acceptance is feeling as if our men understand our hearts. That's why conversation is often the key to a woman's libido. She needs to feel as if she's understood, but she also needs to feel as if all the details bouncing around in her head about her to-do list tomorrow and her worries about the kids are out in the open so that she isn't distracted.

So if you want sex to be great, help her deal with her distractions. Give her alone time earlier in the evening. Talk earlier in the evening so that she feels loved and so she has a chance to process everything that's in her head. And women, if you have a lot of logistic-type worries—like how am I going to manage my time and get everything done?—discuss these with your husband too because he may figure out some activities or tasks you can say no to. Perhaps he can even take responsibility for some of her tasks and reduce her mental load.

Guys, understand that your wife's urge to talk or her need to process is not a rejection of you or a rejection of sex; it's her way of getting her mind in gear and emptied of all her concerns so that she can concentrate and enjoy sex.

Great Sex Challenge 12

Strategize with each other about developing new habits of talking earlier in the evening or giving her alone time earlier in the day while he does the childcare. Then check in with each other about your day. Can you curl up on the couch for fifteen minutes? Can you go for a walk after dinner? When our children were babies, we'd bundle them up, put them into the stroller, and head outside every night to process the day together while the kids were contained. Or you can head to bed earlier and do your processing, talking, and planning then. Keep a day planner near the bed so that together you can go over her calendar and schedule errands in it so she's not worried and distracted. It takes twenty-one days for a habit to become ingrained, so start this one today: find regular, scheduled time just to talk, and if she needs it, regular alone time too.

This may not sound sexy, but before we can move on to how to really enjoy sex, she absolutely must be able to get her head in the game, and that means dealing with the day's stresses. Make this a habit; it will benefit both of you!

JUMP IN!

In movies the couple is usually totally hot for each other, so they fall into bed together. They're both "in the mood." They're both aroused. And so they make love.

That seems honest. They make love *because they want to make love.*

But is it true? Most women just aren't "in the mood" at the drop of a hat, panting and waiting to fall into bed. A *Psychology Today* article explained this well: "That's what University of British Columbia psychiatrist Rosemary Basson, M.D., discovered in interviews with hundreds of women. Contrary to the conventional model, for many women, desire is not the cause of lovemaking, but rather, its result. 'Women,' Basson explains, 'often begin sexual experiences feeling sexually neutral.' But as things heat up, so do they, and they eventually experience desire."[6]

We women need to rethink what being "in the mood" means. Men were designed to need very little stimulation. They see something and they're ready to go. Women, on the other hand, need to relax, to be able to concentrate on what's going on, and then slowly heat up. Some men react more like women; they don't often feel the urge for sex. But feeling the urge first, whether you're male or female, is not a necessary ingredient for making love. Instead, if you just jump in and embrace the thought of showing love and having fun with your spouse, chances are that your body will follow.

To make love when you aren't "in the mood" isn't lying or being dishonest. It's just responding to your spouse. He pursues you and tries to arouse you, then you respond. You love him, so responding to him is an act of love.

If you're male and you're the lower-desire spouse, responding to your wife is even more important. Your wife needs to feel pursued; if you wait until you feel the need for sex, she's going to feel as if something is desperately missing from your relationship.

I'm afraid that many women are missing out on how great sex can be, and what a great sex life they can have, because they think they aren't "in the mood." They believe making love when they don't feel an urgent physical need would somehow be akin to faking. But kissing him when he wants to make love, letting your hands wander, and responding to his wandering hands is not faking. It's *responding*. When you put your head in the game, as Rosemary Basson found, you will tend to heat up.

Now, if you never heat up, you could have low testosterone, and if you never have sexy dreams, never get aroused, and never seem to desire sex, you should be checked for this. On the other hand, he simply may not have learned yet how to properly stimulate you, or perhaps you don't know yourself—we'll look more at that this week. Or you could have some issues with sex, such as past abuse, which you need to seek healing from. But in general, if your husband has learned what your body likes, and you make a decision to respond, your body will indeed likely follow.

It's this decision part that's so important. If you don't make that mental leap that says, "I'm going to throw myself into this and enjoy it," then you likely won't enjoy it very much. You have to turn on your own switch. No matter what he does, he can't arouse you unless you decide to become aroused.

This too makes sense. If women could automatically become

aroused no matter whom they were with, then the pursuit wouldn't be as big a deal, would it? But women don't automatically become aroused; we have to choose to let ourselves, which means we choose to enjoy our husbands. They pursue, and we choose to be caught. Incidentally, this is what men often wish women understood. They desire sex not only, or even primarily, for physical release. Sex is their way of seeing whether we will respond to them and accept them. It's their way of seeing whether we would choose them again. So what really interests a man is not his orgasm nearly as much as his wife's ability—or choice—to respond sexually.

How do you heat up? When you're making love and he's touching you, keep asking yourself, over and over, "Where do I want him to touch now? What feels good?" If you ask these questions, then you're paying attention to your body and you're thinking about what it's feeling. And that, in and of itself, is the key to arousal. You're not letting yourself become distracted; you're thinking about your body. And as you do, you'll likely find that some body part does want to be touched. Just move his hand there and show him! And then the arousal will likely start!

And guys, if you're the lower-libido spouse, when you decide to initiate and to focus on sex and invite her to touch you, chances are your body will respond too. Give yourself time to heat up, and spend a lot of time touching, paying attention to your body's cues. Don't forsake sex just because you don't have the same urge you felt when you were sixteen. She needs to feel like she's desirable, so jump in!

Great Sex Challenge 13

If you're the lower-desire spouse, jump in and initiate sex, even if you don't think you're in the mood. Be the assertive one, the one who starts foreplay, the one who does most of the moving. Decide to enjoy it. Pay attention to what your body is feeling and what your body wants, and see how your body responds.

10 Signs You Should Seek Help for Sexual Problems

1. Sex is painful for her.

Painful sex due to vaginismus is a big part of my story. When I was first married, intercourse was very painful because my vaginal muscles wouldn't relax, leaving me feeling like I was broken. It took several years to train myself to control those muscles. I wish I had had the help then that's available now through pelvic floor physiotherapists. I believe my journey would have been much easier and less emotionally draining.

Many women experience a bit of discomfort during sex, but it's relieved by switching positions or adjusting the depth of penetration. If, however, sex is painful consistently, like it was for me, or if penetration is impossible because of pain or if you have a burning sensation in the vulva, you may be experiencing vaginismus (pain during sex caused by involuntary tightening of the muscles in the vagina), vulvodynia (a pain disorder that causes a burning sensation in the vulva), or dyspareunia (pain during sex, broadly). A variety of treatments are available depending on the cause of the pain you're experiencing. Talk to your doctor, and ask for a referral to a pelvic floor physiotherapist who can help.

2. She has just given birth.

Childbirth is very taxing on her pelvic floor. Many women also experience tearing, which causes scar tissue that needs to be relaxed and stretched. Pelvic floor physiotherapists recommend getting checked out early in the third trimester and after you've given birth to help prevent problems, and also to treat any that come up.

3. She can't orgasm.

If, after going through this whole series and working on making sex feel good for her, she still can't orgasm—especially if it's accompanied by a lack of ability to get aroused in general and a lack of sexual dreams—she may be suffering from anorgasmia. Talk to your doctor to see whether this has hormonal, medical, or pharmaceutic roots.

4. He orgasms too quickly.

While most men can reach orgasm in two to three minutes, most can also extend that time considerably with concentration. Some men, however, orgasm with very little stimulation and are unable to hold it off. This condition is called premature ejaculation, and some treatments and medications can help (along with using a start-and-stop sexual technique). I once spoke with a woman at a marriage conference who told me how she simply didn't enjoy sex, but upon further questioning, it was clear that sex never lasted more than a few minutes. They had been married for twenty-three years and had no idea this wasn't normal! Seek help if his early orgasm is impeding your sexual relationship.

5. You never want sex.

Low libido is extremely common, and in the vast majority of cases, libido is something you can boost by having a better mind-set, cultivating a better relationship, and eating better, all of which are covered in this 31-day challenge. But some people have libido issues that don't improve with these measures. If you never have sexual dreams, if you have difficulty getting aroused, and if you never spontaneously think about sex, you may be experiencing hypoactive sexual desire disorder. Your doctor can help you figure out the cause of your lack of desire and figure out what treatment will work best.

For men, testosterone supplements and shots can help; women are sometimes deficient in another hormone. Some medications, especially antidepressants, can also impede libido. Please don't wait to get this checked out, especially if you're a guy, because the treatment is often relatively simple.

6. He can't establish or sustain an erection.

Erectile dysfunction is a common part of the aging process in men. But erectile dysfunction has also been linked to porn use, and so is increasingly common among younger men. On top of all this, erectile dysfunction is often a sign of heart issues (which is why it's common as men age and circulatory problems develop). No matter how old you are or whether you're in good or bad shape, if you are consistently having difficulty in this area, please see your doctor! This may be a symptom of something much more severe, and it never hurts to get it checked out. If porn is the issue, counseling to deal with the porn addiction and exercises later in this month to improve intimacy may retrain the brain so that the relationship—and not just the porn—is arousing again.

7. Having sex makes you feel sick or sad.

For some people, orgasm causes a variety of symptoms, ranging from headaches to anxiety attacks to depression. I'm not talking about a one-off headache, but instead I'm referring to a persistent symptom that occurs frequently after orgasm. A number of conditions can make people feel ill or even burst into tears after they've experienced orgasm. In women especially, postcoital dysphoria (or experiencing the post-sex blues) is linked to the same hormonal imbalances that cause postpartum depression. Talk to your doctor so they are aware of your elevated risk for PPD, and seek out additional professional help if necessary. Some medications can treat these types of conditions effectively.

8. You are leaking urine or have the urge to "go" frequently but don't have much urine to pass.

Urinary incontinence is an extremely common problem, especially for women. It's often triggered by childbirth or the typical aging process as the pelvic floor muscles weaken. If you leak urine throughout the day, find that you have little "accidents" when you sneeze or jump, or have the urge to pee but don't have anything to pass, ask your doctor about seeing a pelvic floor physiotherapist. It's a treatable condition, and with modern treatment methods, you don't need to keep dealing with the stress and worry that come with incontinence. For men, this can also be a sign of something wrong with the prostate, and getting that checked is crucial for overall health.

9. You experience discomfort, itchiness, or blisters on your genitals.

For women, itchiness could indicate vaginal bacterial infections such as yeast infections or bacterial vaginosis. These are unpleasant and uncomfortable but are easily treated if you deal with them quickly. Itchiness may also indicate a urinary tract infection if you're experiencing a burning sensation when you pee (men can get these too, by the way!).

If you ever notice any sort of blisters, warts, or general abnormalities in the genital region, having a medical professional look at it is always wise. If you or your spouse had past partners and were never tested for STDs before you got married, this is especially urgent as it may be a symptom of an STD. Many sexually transmitted infections and diseases can remain in the system without showing symptoms for long periods of time, so it's always a good idea to see a doctor just to rule it out and to figure out the cause of the discomfort.

10. You hear a "crack" during sex.

I can't emphasize this enough: IF YOU HEAR A CRACK, CALL AN

AMBULANCE AS QUICKLY AS YOU CAN. If you are using a sexual position that puts too much weight on the penis, it is possible for the penis to be badly sprained or even broken and require surgery.

To prevent this, as a general rule, any sort of position where her weight is being held up by his penis is an absolute no-go. Just don't do it. If he wants to be standing during sex, have her weight rest on a surface like a bed or chair. It's not worth the risk to do the positions where he's holding her up—it can turn bad very quickly!

PUT THE "PLAY" IN FOREPLAY!

Yesterday we talked about how most women don't necessarily feel "in the mood" before they begin making love—it's something that comes once they start. But if "starting" means jumping quickly to intercourse, it could be that you're skipping steps that she needs to reach arousal.

So today let's talk about foreplay: what it is, how to make it great, and how to figure out what she likes. Before we do that, let's go over some misconceptions about foreplay.

Foreplay Can Get Too Clinical

If you always follow a formula that says "spend two minutes touching her breasts and then four minutes between her legs," foreplay is hardly going to be fun. It can seem rote—like he's doing it just to get going, sort of like priming an engine before turning it on. And if he aims for an especially sensitive area before you've spent any time kissing or holding each other, it can seem intrusive to her.

For foreplay to be pleasurable, it needs to be part of the whole experience—not just something you have to do and want to get over with so that you can get to the main event.

Touching and exploring each other's bodies should be fun.

Foreplay doesn't always have to involve the same actions for the same amount of time. And if you spend a lot of time in foreplay, your sexual connection can seem much more intimate and can make actual intercourse much more intense.

Foreplay Can Be Too Much of a One-Way Street

If foreplay consists entirely of him touching her (because he's already in the mood, and she's not), then it can make a lot of women feel somehow inferior. *What's wrong with me that I'm not ready?*

Instead, make it about both of you. Women, touch him too so it's about feeling each other and experiencing each other, not just him trying to make her catch up to where he is.

Foreplay Can Become Routine

While certain things feel good to women, if you do too much of the same thing, it can get boring. What really arouses a person is a combination of elements—feeling loved, feeling a little bit teased, having all the nerves firing. You can do that in different ways. Sometimes one of the sexiest things is to have him touch everything, very slowly, except her real erogenous zones. That makes those zones ever so much more sensitive. You don't always have to do the same thing every night. And you don't always have to use just fingers either. Kiss each other. Feel with the whole hand. Rub your hair over him. Be creative. The more you get involved, the more exciting and fun it will be.

Foreplay Can Be Too Rough

Men tend to enjoy being touched intimately much more firmly than women do. Men like to be squeezed, but if a guy touches a woman's erogenous zones the way he likes to be touched, it's going to hurt—or at least be uncomfortable. Many women, when they're new to sex, experience this and think, "I guess I don't like my breasts touched," or "I guess I don't like foreplay." That's not true. Perhaps he just never touched them the way she needs to be touched!

How to Make Foreplay Wonderful

WOMEN: TELL HIM WHAT YOU LIKE

Here's the hardest part, ladies: you have to communicate. If you've been married for quite some time and you've never told him that something he does turns you off, it can be even harder because you're worried about hurting his feelings.

I know this is a sensitive subject, but you must let him know. He likely would love to give you pleasure, but he can't know how you feel unless you tell him. So if he's doing something a little too roughly or not hitting exactly the right place, move his hand and show him. You can even touch yourself and show him what you like.

Sometimes showing him how to touch you is easier if you begin by asking him how he likes to be touched. Experiment a bit and say, "Harder? Softer? More? Less?" If you're asking the questions, he may then return the favor.

WOMEN: BE AN ACTIVE PARTICIPANT

Feel him. Touch him. Change positions. Don't just lie there, waiting for him to turn you on. If you're active, the experience is more intimate and you'll enjoy it more.

DRAG IT OUT TO RELAX YOU

Start with a bath together where you talk about your day and just caress each other. Or try my personal favorite—a massage! Naked massages are especially erotic because while they're not explicitly sexual, they feel wonderful and they're very physical. They give you each time to transition from the worries of the day to the evening. And when you massage naked, it's much more intimate!

Don't Rush It

Finally, don't rush it. Give her proper time to get aroused, and for many women that takes a good fifteen to twenty minutes. If you're each involved and you're relaxed and laughing together too, that's much better than feeling like "because he's been touching me for two minutes, I should be ready to go, so I guess we'll just start," or "I've been touching her for a few minutes, so that ought to do it."

And ladies, if you're not sure what you like, and you've always been nervous about having all the attention during foreplay, I'd challenge you to redo the challenge from day 5 and let him touch your body for fifteen minutes while you sit back and enjoy. In fact, this is a great assignment to do over and over again! It takes the pressure off you if you feel like you should be ready but you're not, and it teaches him to figure out what you like (while also showing *you* what you like).

Remember, foreplay isn't optional. Most women aren't "wet" enough to make love comfortably without some stimulation first. It's not as if intercourse is the main event and everything else is suboptimal. The whole experience is part of sex, not just intercourse. And foreplay is vitally important because it helps focus you not only on your genitals but also on your hands, your eyes, your mouth—everything. In many ways, it's more personal, and even more intimate, than intercourse. So try to ramp up foreplay, and you'll find sex more exciting!

Great Sex Challenge 14

Spend at least fifteen minutes in foreplay. Set the timer, and don't let yourself start intercourse until you've been kissing and exploring for at least fifteen minutes. Throw yourself into it, touch each other, and have fun! Your bodies are yours to explore. Don't shortchange the time!

Turn Foreplay Up a Notch

Yesterday was foreplay day, but it's such an important subject that it deserves another go-around! Here's an email I received from a reader after the initial foreplay challenge on my blog: "My husband really doesn't 'get' foreplay. He thinks foreplay is 'just for me,' while sex is for 'both of us,' and so if I want foreplay I'm being selfish, and I should do what's best for 'both of us.' He doesn't understand that I can't really enjoy intercourse if I don't warm up first."

Part of the reason we often rush foreplay is that it can be awkward. She's lying there, and he's just touching her, and everybody feels like they're watching the clock, secretly saying, *"Why is this taking so long?"* The woman feels as if she's being judged if she doesn't get aroused quickly, and the man feels like we should be getting to the main event.

Yesterday we looked at some ways to make foreplay work better for her. Now here are some ways to make him excited about it too so that both of you can embrace it as a vital part of making love!

Let Him Watch

Men are highly visual, and foreplay can begin with the way women beckon them upstairs or undress or crawl into bed. Push him onto the bed and then let him watch as you take off your clothes. I know some women are sensitive to how their bodies look, but remember that he gets pleasure from it, and your body is the only naked woman's body he's allowed to see. Let him see it!

Besides, what's sexy is not just how your body looks but what you do with it. Ladies, tease him by taking off your undergarments slowly—maybe even while you're leaning over him. Run your hands over your body before you let him touch you. That's the kind of thing that will get him going!

Often the reason we women like to get into our flannel pajamas, rush under the covers, and then get undressed under the covers is because the bedroom is so cold, especially in winter. That's certainly the case in Canada, where I'm from! Keeping the heat lower at night is a great way to conserve energy and save some money. But guys, *if you want to turn up the heat in the bedroom, you might want to actually turn up the heat*. One quick fix is to buy a space heater and put it on her side of the bed.

Touch Him Too

Foreplay doesn't have to be only for her; it can and should also involve her touching him. And touch him everywhere, not just his genitals. Tease him a bit, then ask him to show you just how he likes to be touched or stroked. Women often use too soft of a touch, so just ask him to guide your hand.

Now, touching him the whole time he's stimulating you may not be the best idea since he may not do a thorough job if he's distracted. But doing it a little bit shows that you care about his pleasure too. And it can also be highly arousing! Touch him and realize the power you have over him. He wants you. Revel in that.

Don't Stay Still

One reason we often feel like we should rush foreplay is because sometimes she is just lying there, which makes the whole experience seem a little boring. But there's no reason you both have to lie that way. In fact, there's no reason why you have to be in any single position for an extended period of time. He could sit up, for instance, and then she could sit against him so they're both facing the same direction. Then he can still reach around and stimulate various parts of her body, but it psychologically feels different. Many women find this position a little more comfortable because they're not eye to eye, so it isn't as intensely personal.

Rub against His Body

He'll enjoy this one: if you need to be stimulated a certain way, stimulate yourself. But not with your hand. Use his body instead. Find a way to grind against his leg, or even against his penis without him entering you, that feels delicious. This requires a lot of movement on the woman's part, which is what he'll really enjoy. It makes it seem as if you are eager for his body and as if you are really enjoying it, which will excite him. And if you keep changing positions to get an even better angle, then he's going to get stimulated too.

You can add some tension to the moment by grabbing his hands and forcing him onto his back, where he has to stay. Then say something like, "Now I'm going to use you." Then press up against him in ways that work for you, and forbid him from moving. He'll feel the sexual tension build, right as you're really enjoying yourself.

Kiss

Don't forget to kiss! If you're kissing, then it won't seem as if there's a ticking clock in the background. And you don't have to just kiss each other's mouths. Kiss anything! You can even kiss something innocuous, like his neck or her ears, but try to tease and drive each other crazy while you're doing it.

Talk

Tell each other what feels good—this is especially important for women! Tell him you love him. Comment on what great muscles he has. Remind him of a great time you had last year on your anniversary. Say something sexy! If you're talking, you're showing him that you are enjoying this. You're into this. You're excited about participating. And to men, knowing that their wives are enjoying sex is a real turn-on.

Remember: what stimulates a man is often visual and psychological even more than physical. If she lets him watch her, he'll be excited. And if he feels as if she's excited, having a good time, and working hard to make this wonderful, then he'll be excited too. So foreplay doesn't have to be just about getting her physically stimulated. It can be about getting her in the mood but doing it in a way that also reassures her husband that she's excited about being together. If you do all those things, sex won't seem like the main event anymore. It will seem like it's part of the whole package!

Great Sex Challenge 15

Turn foreplay up a notch! Choose at least three of the ideas mentioned, and do them during foreplay tonight. And I'd recommend the one about rubbing against him to stimulate her. She'll get exactly what she needs, but he'll enjoy the action!

HELP HER REACH THE BIG "O"

After my husband and I gave the "sex talk" at a FamilyLife Canada marriage conference, a very determined woman approached me: "I have a question, and I've never found anyone I could ask. What is an orgasm? And how do I know if I've had one?"

In the surveys I took for *The Good Girl's Guide to Great Sex*, around 61 percent regularly orgasm (either from stimulation or from intercourse), but that leaves 39 percent who don't very often. And some of those 39 percent have never reached orgasm at all.

An orgasm is the height of sexual pleasure. While a man's orgasm is rather obvious, a woman's is not quite as obvoius—though it feels just as good! Women tend to climax right after an exquisite tension when if your husband stopped doing whatever he was doing, you'd likely burst into tears. When women orgasm, waves of pleasure pass over them. Their legs tend to stiffen up. Their heads often turn involuntarily from side to side. And their vaginal muscles contract. Plus, it feels wonderful.

Most women find it easier to orgasm to oral or manual stimulation than they do during intercourse (tomorrow we'll talk about why this is). But what do you do if you've never experienced an orgasm, or if they tend to be rather rare?

First, that's perfectly natural. Women are more likely to orgasm

115

once they've been married for a few years, so if it takes a while, that's okay. Orgasm is the ultimate letting go; if you're still shy early in your marriage, letting go can be difficult. Don't worry about it. The more you worry about it, the less likely you are to get there.

But just because many women take a few years to get there, that doesn't mean you have to! Here are some tips to make orgasm more likely.

Relax

To orgasm, you need to be swept away by the moment and the feeling. If something is distracting you, it's hard to be swept away. That's why if you're tense, it's unlikely to happen. The best thing you can do is relax! Don't worry; it will happen one day once your body is used to pleasure.

Move

Don't lie there, waiting for it to come upon you. Remain an active participant as you make love. Switch positions, even a little bit, so that it feels good. Tilt your body. Move on top sometimes. Take his hand and move it where you'd like to be stimulated, even during intercourse. The more you take the initiative, the sexier you'll feel.

Concentrate on Feeling Good

Here's the most important tip: concentrate on feeling good, not on reaching orgasm. Make pleasure your goal. As you make love, concentrate on the pleasure you're feeling. Ask yourself, "What feels good?" or "Where do I want my husband to touch now?" That helps you zero in on anything arousing. Then slowly let that pleasure carry you away. If what he's doing doesn't feel good, then shift a bit, or position him differently. Let him know; he's likely eager to make the right adjustments!

Breathe

We sometimes stop breathing because we feel like we're oh-so-close. We tense our legs, concentrate hard, and hold our breath. Now, for some women that does work. But for many others, it can bring the crescendo of pleasure to a halt. Without oxygen, orgasm remains elusive. So just like they say in exercise class, don't forget to breathe! If you find yourself stiffening up your legs and stopping your breathing in desperation for the orgasm, and then you can't get there, try the opposite. Relax, breathe deeply, and let the waves of pleasure carry you rather than trying to force them.

A Note to Him

If you put too much pressure on your wife to orgasm, and she feels like a failure if she doesn't, then she's less likely to want to make love if she thinks she may not reach climax. It's great to want to pleasure her; but pressuring her can often backfire. Just take things slowly, laugh a lot, leave time to explore, and let things happen.

Now, if you're consistently reaching climax before she does, please don't leave her hanging. Make it a habit to help her afterward by stimulating her clitoris or anything else she finds pleasurable. If she's consistently left sexually frustrated, that will increase her tension about not being able to reach orgasm and may make it more difficult to climax.

Great Sex Challenge 16

Redo yesterday's challenge to concentrate on foreplay and then take it one step further. If she's never experienced an orgasm, try to prolong foreplay to see if it happens. If you're up for it, *don't give up until it happens!* Some couples have tried this, even if it takes hours, and the relief is immense. Women, concentrate on the pleasure, concentrate on what your body is feeling, and relax. If she has experienced orgasm through ways other than intercourse but has a hard time achieving one through intercourse, spend a ton of time on foreplay, and start intercourse only when she's very close to climax. And ladies, learn to revel in the pleasure.

THE PLEASURE CENTER

"I just don't understand what the big deal is about sex." I hear that from women all the time. People may look breathless in movies, but sex sure doesn't take these women's breath away.

Today we're going to try to show her what the big deal is! Many women simply have not experienced sex as feeling physically wonderful. After all, it's kind of tricky for us because we're not guaranteed pleasure the way men usually are.

Once women experience the pleasure that can make sex much more passionate, frequency of sex increases. But the passion itself is what the husbands often crave. It's not just the release; it's seeing her receive and experience pleasure.

How can we experience pleasure? We've talked about spending more time on foreplay and how to relax and experience orgasm, but let's get a little more technical (which will lead to more fun!).

Here's the thing about orgasm for women: pretty much all orgasms are caused by the clitoris (that little knob of flesh in front of the vagina) being stimulated or pressed. The vagina itself doesn't have that many nerves; the clitoris, as tiny as it is, actually has more nerves than the penis. The clitoris is the little bundle of pleasure.

But because it's little, it often doesn't get a lot of stimulation once intercourse starts. So here are a few tips for making sure your clitoris gets the attention it needs to experience real pleasure.

Change Up the Missionary Position

Ladies, tilt your pelvis up when you're on the bottom. If he's on top and you just lie there, you won't experience a lot of stimulation. Tilt up, though, and you'll put pressure on the clitoris and change the angle so that his pelvic bone stimulates you during intercourse. So try tilting up (just by squeezing your butt muscles, so to speak). It's a little change, but it does a lot! Just by squeezing your muscles, you'll engage the clitoris, and that will feel better in and of itself.

Put Her on Top

Make love with her on top. Then have her slowly change the angle so she can hit him at the spot that makes her feel good. Just keep adjusting or rotating gradually until it feels good.

Touch Her during Intercourse

If you try positions other than the missionary position, have him put a finger or two on her clitoris so that she receives stimulation during intercourse. During foreplay she may feel great because he directly stimulates her where it's very pleasurable, but then you start intercourse, and the stimulation almost stops, depending on your position. If he can still provide pressure with his fingers, that can keep the momentum going.

One little tip for guys: don't concentrate on rubbing her clitoris during intercourse; just put your finger there. The pressure is all she needs, and with you thrusting so much, you're likely to rub a little too roughly. It's better to just provide pressure than to try to do much else.

Many women feel as if something must be wrong with them because intercourse itself just doesn't feel that wonderful. But that's quite normal. Because the vagina doesn't have many nerves, unless you make an effort to have her clitoris line up with the base of his pelvis, she isn't going to get the pleasurable feeling she needs. Nothing is wrong with her. You both just need to adjust your position a bit!

I received an email from a woman that said: "I'm always hearing about all kinds of different positions, and I do want to have a fun and varied sex life! But to tell you the truth, there's really only one position that works for me. I can't orgasm any other way. What's wrong with me?"

Absolutely nothing. Most women reach orgasm much more easily through stimulation other than intercourse—and there may be only one or two positions for intercourse where the angle gives enough stimulation. Usually women have to rotate and tilt to get that angle just right. And it's not the same position for each woman either! If you enjoy other positions but find that only one lets her orgasm, that's okay. You can always use the others as foreplay and then finish in your favorite. If she doesn't benefit from sexual gymnastics, that doesn't mean she's inferior!

Incidentally, as you women try to find the right position, it also means you have to be more active while you make love. You have to shift a bit, or tilt a bit, and that means you'll be more engaged. Your husband will likely appreciate this because it will show that you want to make love and that you are choosing to receive pleasure. That's a big deal to a man. So even if it takes you a few tries (or a lot of tries) to find an angle that provides a lot of pleasurable sensations, he'll enjoy your effort (and likely so will you).

And if, at the end of that, she still can't orgasm through intercourse, but only can through other stimulation, that doesn't mean you've failed! As long as you're both enjoying yourself and feeling close, you're fine. Just make sure she reaches orgasm in some way, even if it's not through intercourse, because sex is meant to be mutual.

Great Sex Challenge 17

Tonight, try a position or two, but let her lead. Give her time to rotate to experiment with getting the angle right. This takes some courage and assertiveness. She'll have to speak up! And if it doesn't feel right, keep trying. Change positions if you have to. But don't just "settle" for something. Ladies, tell him what feels good, and keep working at it until you find the perfect position!

The Theology of the Clitoris

I remember being in shock at a youth group retreat where the pastor referred to the clitoris. His point was that *God created a part of a woman's body that's only purpose is for her sexual pleasure.*

At the time I wanted the floor to open and swallow me up. I didn't know what to do with that information. In retrospect, I'm glad he pointed out the purpose of the clitoris because two thoughts stuck with me:

- Sex isn't just about the guy feeling good.
- God intended for sex to be pleasurable.

That's what that pastor wanted us all to know, and he was so right. We don't need to feel awkward for enjoying sex or embarrassed about wanting sex, because God made sex to be pleasurable. So let's look at what the clitoris can tell us about what God intends for sex, how God feels about women, and even what we can learn about God in general.

WHAT THE CLITORIS TELLS US ABOUT SEX

God created a body part that is only for pleasure. The penis has several purposes, but the clitoris is for only one thing. That means sex is supposed to be pleasurable in general but also specifically for women. God intended sex to be specifically for women's sexual pleasure too.

What's really interesting, I think, is the location of the clitoris—between the folds of skin just in front of the opening of the vagina. The most natural way for the clitoris to get some attention is when the couple is face-to-face. Either he's manually stimulating her, or they're having intercourse in some position where they're face-to-face. That's not to say you can't use other positions; but the fact that the clitoris is often stimulated when you're facing each other means *God intended for sex to be personal*. Pretty much all other animals have sex from a rear entry position. But God shows that humankind is different. He intended sex to be about both of you feeling close. One of the most intimate things you can do is to look into each other's eyes at the height of orgasm, when the oxytocin (the bonding hormone) is at its peak. It bonds you!

WHAT THE CLITORIS TELLS US ABOUT GENDER DYNAMICS

God could have made women's bodies so that we get maximum pleasure from intercourse. But he didn't. That doesn't mean women can't feel pleasure from intercourse, but in general, most women report that they reach orgasm easier from clitoral stimulation. They tend to need a lot of manual or oral stimulation first if they're going to reach orgasm through intercourse.

Why did God make the clitoris this way? Here's my theory: while men often reach climax quite quickly through intercourse alone, women don't. That means that for women to feel pleasure, men have to slow down and think about their wives. Sex is best when it isn't just "animal" style, where you simply have intercourse with no foreplay, because that won't feel good for her. Men have to learn to be unselfish if sex is going to work well for both partners. Women tend to feel like they're the ones always serving others, but God deliberately made our bodies so that if we're going to feel good during sex, men have to take time to serve women.

WHAT THE CLITORIS TELLS US ABOUT WHAT GOD WANTS FOR WOMEN

Here's something interesting: while sex works best when the man doesn't think about what he's feeling but concentrates on what she's feeling (so as to prolong intercourse and to make her feel good), it also works best when the woman *does* think about what she's feeling. She has to stop multitasking, stop thinking about anything else, and just let herself feel. That's hard for women to do because we're so used to thinking about what everyone else needs. But for sex to work well, we have to be a little selfish. We have to pay attention to what's going on in our bodies.

God made sex as a gift for women, when we have to slow down and just feel.

WHAT THE CLITORIS (AND ORGASM) TELLS US ABOUT GOD

The fact that women have a clitoris means God desires orgasm to be part of the female experience too. What does that teach us about God? It shows that God does not intend for us always to feel in control. We can't orgasm if we're trying to control everything. We have to let go and let it happen. And orgasm itself is the antithesis of thought. Sometimes you can't think straight when you're having an orgasm. It's almost like something else is carrying you along.

That's what God wants women to know about passion: we don't always have to be in control. God created sex as a mirror for what our lives with him are supposed to be like. He doesn't want us to feel always in control. He wants us, sometimes, to just be carried along by him, to just trust and experience love and feel joy.

That's pretty cool for one little body part. Think about it:

- God wants women to experience pleasure.
- God wants that pleasure to be both intimate and personal.
- God wants husbands to pay attention to and take time to please their wives.
- God wants women not to feel like they always have to be the ones giving but to learn how to receive.
- God wants us to learn not to multitask sometimes and not to always feel in control but to let ourselves be carried along.

Women, that's what God wants for you.

Do you understand that?

That tells me that God loves women—that God cares about us and designed sex to be something wonderful for us.

I don't know where you are today. Maybe you're someone for whom sex has never felt that great. Maybe you feel beaten down by God, as though he likes your husband better. Maybe you feel like sex is great for everyone but you.

Review that list again, and remind yourself that this is honestly God's heart for you. Sex is a gift he designed for you. You aren't an afterthought, where you get the crumbs your husband leaves behind. You're important. That's how God sees you. And that's amazing.

LITTLE CHANGES THAT FEEL AMAZING FOR HER

Sometimes the smallest changes can make the biggest impact! Yesterday we talked about her tilting her pelvis to achieve more stimulation where it's needed; today we're going to list some things men can do to make sex feel that much better for her. Guys, here we go.

Let the Tension Build

Teasing and building tension often make sex far more pleasurable for women than just jumping in, because the teasing helps her anticipate what's coming. Since sex for women is so much in our heads, we need the chance to look forward!

When you're making love, then, don't thrust all the way in at the start. Start shallow and slow, growing more deliberate and deeper as she starts to feel more aroused. Sometimes, of course, she'll like things done more quickly, but encourage her to set the pace. If you start right in before she's ready, she often will never have a chance to catch up.

Use Lubrication When Needed

Some women have a hard time "getting wet." And when you're not well-lubricated, sex doesn't feel good. But if you add some lubrication, which is readily available at the drugstore, she'll feel more pleasure. And save the ones that change temperature or give extra sensation for special nights. A simple lubricant with no bells or whistles (or menthol tingles) can make sex much more pleasurable.

Lubricant should never replace foreplay, but at times it can be handy, such as when trying a new position, when enjoying a "quickie," or even when going through menopause when hormones are all over the place.

Pay Attention to Her Breasts

Breasts are funny things; some women enjoy their nipples being stimulated, and some don't. But just because she doesn't like it during foreplay doesn't mean she won't like it later. Often women whose nipples are sensitive when they aren't very aroused actually enjoy being pinched a bit right before orgasm. So experiment a little. The best way to tell is for her to be aware of her own body. Ladies, pay attention to your body's cues; chances are it will give you signals. So ask yourself, "What wants to be touched now?" You may find that your breasts respond later, near the end of the encounter! Then make sure to tell him.

Locate Her G-Spot

Finally we have the elusive G-spot. Yesterday I said that what triggers almost all orgasms is clitoral stimulation, and that's mostly true. But many women also swear by the "G-spot," a little oval of flesh that's more "knobby" than usual located about 1½ to 3 inches up the front wall of the vagina (the wall that's against your stomach, not your back). The root of the G-spot is not right at the surface but about half an inch below, so it's a little difficult to stimulate. Also, because it's below the surface of the front wall, it can be difficult to find when you're in the missionary position. Some researchers believe the G-spot is simply an extension of the clitoris, with clitoral "roots" extending up the wall of the vagina. Others think it doesn't exist at all.

My feeling is that we should never feel dysfunctional if we can't find it, since large-scale studies have failed to consistently show a definite anatomical location for it. But many women swear by it, and since any research you do to find the G-spot is bound to be fun, why not try? It will feel good even if you don't find it.

You can try to locate the G-spot either by having him insert his fingers (after applying lubricant!) or through intercourse. Some people find that the "spooning" position, where you're lying on your sides facing the same direction, and the woman-on-top position, so she can vary her movement, work best. You'll know when you find it; it's often an intense rush, with orgasm soon afterward.

Great Sex Challenge 18

Pick one or two of the items from today, and try to do them tonight. And don't limit yourself to what's here. Guys, ask her what she thinks would make sex feel amazing for her, because she may have some ideas she's been afraid to share. Don't take it personally if she asks you to do something differently; just take it to mean she's committed to improving your sex life. And ladies, open up and let him know what you want or what you'd like to try. The sky's the limit!

The G-Spot

What is the G-spot? The term, named after German gynecologist Ernst Gräfenberg, was made popular in the 1980s. It's about 1½ inches up the front wall of the vagina (the same side as your belly button, not your back). Originally it was thought to be about a one-inch-square size bit of flesh.

The first people to write about the G-spot said it caused intense vaginal orgasms and, in some cases, "female ejaculation," where at orgasm she suddenly "squirts" some liquid. When this happens, many women are afraid that they just urinated, but that's not the case at all. This has been documented for hundreds of years in some pretty scary old medical books for some pretty scary treatments (as you can imagine), but there's no doubt that female ejaculation can happen.

In the 1990s an explosion of articles tried to teach women how to locate their G-spot. Women's magazines in the 1990s and early 2000s routinely included articles about this "new" thing that had just been learned, and they helped women try to reach new heights of pleasure.

The problem was that a lot of women couldn't find a specific spot. They were reading all these articles saying, "It's there! You should find it!" But sex itself didn't seem to be able to stimulate it. So researchers also jumped in the game and tried to find a specific spot. They couldn't, and when they released their study saying that the G-spot didn't exist, they got all kinds of pushback from women saying, "But it does! I can feel it!"

SO WHAT'S THE TRUTH ABOUT THE G-SPOT?

What many researchers now believe is that the G-spot isn't a specific spot as much as it is a region on the front wall of the vagina, on the other side of the urethral sponge (which is often why sex can feel better when you have a slight urge to urinate). And the G-spot is not a separate entity but rather the result of "roots" of the clitoris. They think the clitoris has "legs," or roots, that extend up the front wall of the vagina when aroused and that this can cause far more intense orgasms than the clitoris alone.

Some women seem to be far more sensitive in that area than others, and it seems to be because of the thickness of the tissue in the area. It's something scientists are still trying to figure out.

WHAT DOES THIS MEAN FOR YOU?

No one should feel like they have to find a G-spot or that they're somehow inadequate if they don't. Even women who say they have a G-spot often have a difficult time experiencing orgasm through "missionary position" sex because the penis just isn't putting pressure on the right place at the right angle.

Remember that if she tilts her pelvis while you're making love, and clenches her bottom a bit, she's more likely to activate some of those nerve endings on the front wall of the vagina. She gets her body in a better position, her muscles are activated, and a bit of pressure is put on that urethral sponge, which can push down on that region and feel better.

So here's the tip: during intercourse in any position, get comfortable. Once you are, tilt your hips a bit. Then try making circles instead of thrusting, and see if it feels more delicious!

Little Changes That Feel Amazing for Him

Guys don't usually have as much trouble feeling physical pleasure from sex as women do, but that doesn't mean there aren't small changes women can make to help him feel even more amazing. So, ladies, here are a few tips to make sex extra special for him.

Move

Too often we women can fall into the trap of thinking that what really matters to a guy is sexual release: he needs his orgasm, then he's fine. But remember that to a man, sexuality is wrapped up in his whole identity. Sexual release isn't all he needs; he requires the feeling of acceptance and love that he gets from knowing that his wife wants to make love to him. She doesn't just *let* him; she *wants* him.

For a guy to feel great, then, you need to show him that you enjoy sex too! So much of his pleasure is wrapped up in the idea that he can make you feel so good your toes curl. So don't just lie there. Move! Run your hands over his back. Try a new position. Respond to his thrusting by moving your hips. Show that you're into it.

Vocalize

Don't just move; moan. Or talk. Or say something! Guys love hearing feedback that what they're doing feels good. It doesn't need to sound particularly "dirty" either. Saying, "Oh, I love that," or "Don't stop!" can go a long way in making him feel amazing.

Remember His Erogenous Zones

Women have lots of sensitive areas. We tend to focus on more areas of a woman's body during sex than of a man's because she needs the attention to get aroused during foreplay. But in so doing, we can shortchange the guys. Contrary to common belief, men do have more than one erogenous zone. Many men find their nipples sensitive, and also their necks and earlobes or behind their knees. So pay attention to other parts of his body too, especially his ears and neck, when you make love. This will make it more intimate and intense for him.

Squeeze Him

While the ego boost of showing him you're enjoying sex is awesome, a few physical acts can send him to ecstasy as well. One of the most pleasurable things you can do is to squeeze him while he's inside you, using your pelvic muscles, which can open and contract your vagina. You may not have noticed them before, but if you stop the flow of urine when you're peeing, you're activating the same muscles.

When you make love, just do that same movement and squeeze him. You can hold the squeeze, or if your muscles are strong, you can squeeze rhythmically to his thrusting. To get used to using these muscles, have him enter you, but then stay still. You can practice squeezing and relaxing, squeezing and relaxing, and see if he notices the difference.

Let Him Go Deeper

Another thing that's especially pleasurable is to find a position that lets him thrust even more deeply. This isn't something to try when you're just getting used to making love or when you're sore. But if you're ready, wrap your legs around his back or even rest your feet on his shoulders (if you're flexible enough).

Now, guys, if she's doing this, she's making herself really vulnerable (which, of course, is part of what makes it exciting). Treat her well, and make sure she isn't uncomfortable. Go slowly at first!

Great Sex Challenge 19

Talk together about which of these ideas he'd like to try (and if he wants to try the more adventurous physical ones, take two days to tackle this challenge!). Guys, here's the night to let her know what it means to you for her to enjoy sex too. Explain to her how you feel when you know she's excited to make love. And let her know what sorts of things she can do or say to reassure you when you make love.

If you want to try the more physical suggestions, take it slowly and learn together. Then show her some appreciation for stretching her limits.

The Theology of the Penis

So what do we learn about God and God's design for sex from how the male anatomy works?

SEXUAL ATTRACTION IS NATURAL

First, at its most basic, intercourse works only if the man is aroused. So God created men to be quite easily aroused (in general). If you compare bell curves of women's libidos and men's libidos, you'll find that they overlap, with men's libidos, in general, being higher. This doesn't mean there aren't women with higher libidos than men; but men tend to have an easier time getting aroused and staying aroused than women do.

This is the way we were designed! Most men naturally feel sexual attraction. It is not a sin. They're wired to be attracted to women sexually so that intercourse is easier. If men were as hit-and-miss regarding arousal and sexual response as women are, then sex would be far less frequent and far more disrupted.

(Again, this is not to say some men don't suffer from sexual dysfunction or low libido, only that *in general* men's arousal is more automatic than women's.)

We should stop framing sexual attraction as a sin. Noticing is not lusting. A man can notice that a woman is beautiful and then do absolutely nothing else with that thought. If we tell men that every time they notice a beautiful woman, they're in sin, we put men in an impossible situation. Noticing a beautiful woman and then imagining her naked or fantasizing is lusting; noticing a beautiful woman but not dwelling on it whatsoever is not a sin at all.

SEX, FOR MEN, IS ABOUT BEING ACCEPTED AND "LET IN"

While women can have sex when they don't want to (which is tragic for too many women), men tend to need to be "into it" to perform. (This doesn't mean men can't be raped; bodies can respond to stimulation even if it's unwanted, a phenomenon called arousal nonconcordance.) But in a relationship, in general, men can't have sex unless they want to. What many men are looking for, then, is a woman who *also* wants to have sex. Good husbands want to be wanted; they don't want to be placated. Sex is about a man entering a woman's body and leaving part of him there. It's the physical symbol of him being accepted. Her wanting sex means she wants *him*. She wants to experience his desire and his excitement, and she wants to be the object of it. When she is enthusiastic about sex, he feels wanted and accepted.

SEX REQUIRES MEN, IN GENERAL, TO WOO WOMEN

Men feel arousal quite easily and often quite intensely, but they also have the need to feel accepted (literally "let in"). For this to happen, women have to actually want them. Certainly a bad man can force a woman to have sex, but that only satisfies lust and a craving for power; it doesn't satisfy the emotional need to be accepted. A man's libido and easy arousal, then, become a God-given impetus to woo his wife. If he wants his wife to be eager to make love, he needs to build the relationship and the emotional connection so that she is willing to be vulnerable with him. His libido, when channeled correctly, feeds a more intimate relationship.

MEN'S AREA OF GREATEST PLEASURE IS ALSO THEIR AREA OF GREATEST VULNERABILITY

Men's genitalia is the focus of the greatest pleasure they can feel—but it is also their most vulnerable point. Want to bring a man to his knees? Kick him you-know-where. Every basic self-defense course teaches women this strategy. Go for the testicles!

Why is that? I suggest that it's to remind men that this part of them can all too easily dominate their relationships, and their attempts to dominate women can also become their biggest downfall. It's to remind them that they are vulnerable. They need to use their bodies correctly, or they risk being hurt, and hurting others.

MEN NEED TO STAY IN CONTROL—OF THEMSELVES

If men want to avoid this vulnerability, they need to stay in control—of themselves. If sex is going to go well, a man can't let himself get carried away. He has to think of the woman who is with him to make sure that she is enthusiastic, enjoying herself, and accepting him. He has to make sure he doesn't overpower or coerce her in any way, which is all too easy to do.

Sex can become like a conquest—he dominates her and she submits to him. But for sex to be all he wants it to be, with a partner who accepts him and is enthusiastic, it must be so much more. That means, for a man, not allowing his instincts to run wild. He must instead temper them with love, with deliberation, with generosity. Those things help the stronger look out for the weaker, and it makes sex far more about giving than it otherwise could be.

Pep Talk #3

For so many people, sex has become a difficult part of their lives. It's become twisted or dirty or shameful or simply nonexistent. I read many responses to my blog and think, "Why are we letting something that God made to be beautiful become a negative thing in our lives? Why are we settling for that? We mustn't let something beautiful be stolen from us anymore."

If you're not having any of these thoughts, feel free to move on to day 20. If you are having these doubts, I understand. But I ache for you.

When the beauty of making love is stolen from you, marriage becomes sad and barren. One of the telltale signs that something is from God is that it is *alive*. Life is from God. And so the opposite—death—is not from God. Think about this: when evil triumphs, it's not usually categorized by luscious trees or plants or beauty. It's ugly. Even if it starts out beautiful, ugliness eventually takes over.

When the Mongols rampaged across Asia and the Middle East in the thirteenth century, they left behind them devastation—and desert. Many places that were not formerly deserts became deserts over the next few decades because the Mongols burned everything. Without plants, the land dried up. Destruction kills what was alive.

If history analogies don't work for you, then think about *The Lord of the Rings*, and compare Mordor with the Shire. The Shire is alive; when Sauron took over Mordor, he made sure everything that was living died (except for his minions also bent on destruction).

I noticed this phenomenon in 1989 when I visited East Berlin. West Berlin was beautiful, with trees and parks and art and lovely buildings; East Berlin was Spartan. Everything was utilitarian. Joy was gone. Evil doesn't just propagate evil; it also tries to destroy that which is beautiful.

Recently I read in my devotions the story of Ezekiel and the dry bones, found in Ezekiel chapter 37. God calls on Ezekiel to prophesy over dead bones, and as he does, the bones rattle. They form together. Sinews grow on them. Then flesh. But they're still dead until God breathes into them.

I think that's a picture of where many of us are today when it comes to sex. We feel dead. We're not excited about it. It doesn't grow our relationship; it eats away at it. So what's our response?

This story makes two points: one, those bones listened to Ezekiel's prophecy and joined together and grew. But second, they weren't fully alive until God breathed into them. (I know I'm taking liberties with it here, but bear with me!)

So what does that mean for you?

LISTEN TO THE TRUTH

God wants you to be *alive*. With God, life is teeming, abundant, lush, tropical, beautiful. If your sex life is not like that, God wants it to be!

Then agree with God! You're not agreeing because you're already experiencing that life; you may very well not be experiencing much of anything. But agree with God that he meant your sex life to be alive. Agree with your spouse, the two of you together, that this is how God wants it to be. And let me say a word to the spouse, whether it's the husband or wife, who has the lower libido: you need to believe this too. *God has so much more for you.* He did not design you this way. He wants your marriage to be alive and fun and passionate. If you feel inadequate, don't shrug your shoulders and say, "Oh well, there's nothing I can do. That's just the way I am." That is a cop-out.

If you are severely overweight, you don't just say, "That's just the way I am." You say, "I need to lose some weight, even if it's hard." If you are consumed by nightmares because of what was done to you in the past, you don't just say, "I guess I'll never sleep again," you get help. And yet somehow, when it comes to sex, we seem content to say, "I guess this is just the way I am."

No, it's not! God wants you to be fully alive and passionate. If you're not there, at least agree with God that having a flourishing sex life is his design.

MOVE TOGETHER TO MAKE IT HAPPEN

Once you've agreed, you've got to actually take steps forward. Those bones started joining together. Sinews were formed. So *do* something! That may mean going back to the beginning of this book and rereading some of the challenges. It may mean going over some of the more difficult ones and really putting your heart into it. Instead of balking and saying, "That's not for me," it may mean admitting, "It scares me a little; it pushes me out of my comfort zone; but I know God wants me to experience passion, so I'm going to try." It may even mean making an appointment to see a licensed counselor (see the appendix) to deal with some of your baggage. Just take a step in the right direction.

LET GOD IN

Here's the final and most important part. You can agree with God all you want. You can try to get things going in the right direction. But ultimately you can't do this by yourself. You can't *will* yourself to be passionate.

God breathed life into those dry bones.

All of us need a breath from God today—even those of us who don't feel particularly bad about our sex lives. All of us need more passion. And when we let God in and feel closer to him and let him work, we will feel so much more alive, both spiritually and sexually. When we feel dry spiritually, we often feel dry sexually. The opposite is also true.

If you want to be fully alive and fully passionate, you need to be passionate about God first. When that relationship is secure, it will have major ripple effects in the bedroom.

PEP TALK CHALLENGE

Pray as a couple. Take each other's hands, and earnestly pray together for your sex life and your spiritual life. Pray that God will breathe passion into you that will be felt in the bedroom and also outside the bedroom. Pray that you will know the feeling of being fully alive in him. And don't just pray quick prayers; wrestle in prayer before God.

Maybe you have a hard time praying as a couple. That's okay! But try to pray for at least a few minutes. Pray about your kids. Pray about your friends. As you come together spiritually, you will feel more connected. And as you ask God together, united, for him to bless your sex life, that prayer will be powerful. So pray—and see God work.

If you're not comfortable praying or aren't religious, you can journal together or talk together or take a walk in nature together. Even write a mission statement of what you want your marriage to be. But if you can pray, please do so. God, who created sex, can also make it stupendous!

True Oneness in the Bedroom

(Spiritual Intimacy)

EXPERIENCING SPIRITUAL ONENESS WHEN YOU MAKE LOVE

In many ways today's challenge is the most important one of this book: I want to explore how sex is supposed to be a true spiritual union—so much more than just something fun and physical.

When I was growing up in church, the King James Version of the Bible was the translation we used—that version with all the "thous" and "thees" and "whithersoevers." While that translation can sometimes obscure the meaning of a passage if we're not familiar with the words or phrases, sometimes that old English can provide a bolt of insight.

I specifically remember hearing a passage from Genesis read out loud one Sunday when I was in junior high: "Adam knew Eve his wife; and she conceived" (Genesis 4:1).

At the time, my friends and I all giggled and elbowed each other because we thought it was so funny. Instead of saying a word that meant "sex," the Bible said "knew." Obviously God was embarrassed by the real word.

But hold on a second. What if something else was going on?

In Psalm 139:23, David says, "Search me, God, and know my heart." In fact, that theme, begging God to dig deep inside our hearts and really "know" us, appears throughout Scripture. And the same Hebrew word is used to represent our deep longing for a union with God and the sexual union between a husband and a wife.

What if there's a connection? What if sex isn't just supposed to be a physical union but is also supposed to encompass this deep longing to be known in every way?

I think that's part of God's plan for sex. In sex we bare ourselves physically. But for sex to work well, we also have to bare ourselves emotionally. We have to be vulnerable. We have to "let go." A woman has to emotionally let him in to even get aroused. A man also has to let his guard down to experience the kind of love he longs for.

God created people with a desperate longing for relationship. We long to know and to be known, and in that knowing to be accepted. It's our deepest need. God gave us this drive to know him and to be known by him, but he also gave us sexual longings that mirror how we long to be truly united with our spouses and with God—to be truly and wonderfully *known*.

It's this spiritual intimacy that people crave most. When we focus only on the physical, sex can often seem shallow. But when we combine the physical with the emotional and the spiritual, sex is breathtaking because it encompasses all that we are.

In contrast to intimate sex, our culture embraces pornographic sex. It is self-focused, about the quest for orgasm rather than relationship. It has also become more debased, with rough sex, violent sex, and degrading sex becoming more and more mainstream in the search for that physical high. Sex in our hooking-up culture can feel empty because it's missing the vital emotional connection. That makes the tremendous high much harder to attain. Since commitment seems so foreign to the way our culture sees sex, the only answer to find that elusive high is to try more and more extreme things.

We who are married have the real deal. We have the ingredients for an amazing sexual relationship because it's real intimacy, not just orgasm. (And by the way, that makes orgasm even better!) In fact, the women who were the most likely to orgasm in the surveys I took were married Christian women. When you're in a lifelong committed relationship, you're more likely to experience *all* the great aspects of sex—including the physical ones.

But how, practically, can we experience "spiritual intimacy" while making love?

Take Time to Be Naked

Don't just take your clothes off to make love. Be naked together. Hold each other. Take a bath together. Even pray together naked! Redo that exercise where you just take time touching each other's bodies. It's more vulnerable to be naked while someone touches you than to be naked only while you "have sex." Take that time to explore!

Take Time to Be *Spiritually* Naked

This may sound weird, but trust me: pray before sex—or at least read a psalm or something. When we unite together spiritually first, it's as if our souls are drawn together. And when our souls are drawn together, we want to draw together in a deeper way. So keep a Bible by the bed and read passages together at nighttime. Try to pray together. If you're uncomfortable with free-form prayer, buy a book of prayers, use a daily prayer app, or try the Anglican daily prayer. When you're sincere and you bow before God together, you are drawn toward each other in a much more intense way.

Look into Each Other's Eyes

The eyes are windows, and yet how often do we close our eyes during sex, as if we're trying to shut the other person out, and concentrate on ourselves? I know sometimes you have to close your eyes to feel everything, but occasionally open them and look into each other's eyes. To actually see your spouse—and to let your spouse see into you—is very intimate, especially at the height of passion.

Say I Love You

While you're making love, or even when you orgasm, say I love you. Make sex about not only feeling good but also expressing love. Say your spouse's name. Show them that you're completely captivated.

Desire Your Spouse

Spiritual intimacy during sex ultimately depends on the desire to be united with your spouse. And that desire is fed throughout the day—by concentrating on what you love about each other, by thinking about each other, by flirting and playing together, by making positive statements about each other to friends. It isn't something that "just happens." It's the culmination of a relationship you already have.

For many couples, a lack of spiritual oneness is the major roadblock to sex being everything it can be. Tomorrow we'll dissect some of the challenges to spiritual intimacy and sex a little more, but I think many people have bought into the idea that sex is only physical, when actually sex is the physical expression of a deep drive we have to be connected to each other.

I recently received this comment from a woman: "I always thought, 'Oh, sex is just something HE needs. I can do fine without it.' So not true. I need it too! We have connected in amazing ways, in and out of the bedroom, and I am so excited to have my old husband back!"

So let's unlock that key to true desire by discovering real oneness. Concentrate on what you love about each other. Pray together. Memorize each other's bodies. Say I love you. Look into each other's eyes. Truly be joined. There is nothing else like it.

Great Sex Challenge Day 20

Before you join together tonight, get emotionally vulnerable with each other. That may sound intimidating, but it doesn't have to be! Just let your spouse in on more of what's going on in your heart and mind. Here's how:

1. Start by sharing your "high" and "low" of the day.

   Tell each other the time today when you felt most powerful, in the groove, on fire. Then share when you felt the most defeated or frustrated. You don't have to share your entire day, but share the big emotional moments.

2. Then ask each other this question: What is a dream you have that you're afraid you won't accomplish?

   Give your spouse time to answer without interrupting. Don't try to fix anything. Just listen.

3. Finally, think back to your childhood, and finish this sentence with your spouse: The one person I wish you could have known from my childhood is . . .

   Perhaps it's someone who died, or perhaps it's someone you've lost touch with. But choose someone who had a big impact on you that your spouse never knew. Now share a memory and what that person meant to you.

After you've shared these thoughts, you've been emotionally vulnerable. You've let each other in. Now it's time to make love, not just have sex. Tonight, while you connect, do your best to show your spouse how much you love them.

BE MENTALLY PRESENT WHEN YOU MAKE LOVE

Feeling totally one with your spouse is a beautiful thing. It's an intense experience, and that intensity often makes the physical side of sex even better.

But many couples struggle to achieve oneness, partly because many people aren't mentally present when they make love. If you're thinking of something else during intercourse or stimulation, your body is responding to fantasy, not reality. Your spouse isn't capturing your attention; an image from a movie or a book or pornography or even a memory is. That wrecks intimacy.

Unfortunately, in our pornographic culture, sex has often been reduced to the physical. A person isn't arousing; an image is. And so we find it difficult to get aroused during sex without first concentrating on a mental image. Psychologists have even coined a new term, Sexual Attention Deficit Disorder, for when someone can't maintain an erection, or can't stay aroused, with their spouse but requires additional stimulus, like porn or erotica.

My husband is a physician, and when he was in medical school, he was taught that when you counsel a couple having sexual problems, you should recommend that they watch porn together. Porn has become mainstream. Yet it is not harmless. The more that our bodies become aroused by external stimulus, like pornography, the more our bodies require that stimulus to become aroused. The feeling—arousal—is now associated primarily with that stimulus. So just being with your spouse and touching your spouse isn't enough anymore.

To compound the problem, when people use pornography (and it isn't just men; 30 percent of porn users are female), they usually masturbate as well. They spend their sexual energy on pornography rather than on their marriage. That diminishes their desire for their spouse and is one of the leading causes of lack of libido.

While many women also use porn, our temptation often leans toward erotica. Novels like *Fifty Shades of Grey* sell like hotcakes to sexually frustrated moms, and people think it's harmless. It's simply getting her in the mood! And that's good, right?

Nope. While she may be in the mood, she's in the mood *because of a fantasy*, not because of her husband. When she makes love, it's that fantasy that turns her on, not her husband. The more we use an external stimulus to get aroused, the less our spouse will be able to arouse us, and the more difficulty we will have staying "mentally present" while we make love.

Now, remembering something you and your spouse did together that led to earth-shattering orgasms or imagining something you'd like to do together or even imagining yourself on a beach can be fun and a libido booster. But to fantasize about someone who isn't your spouse or to use pornographic images to get aroused isn't right. You're not there experiencing something with your spouse; you're off on your own, and you're essentially using your spouse as you fantasize.

For sex to be intimate, we can't replay a fantasy or pornography. We need to stay mentally present. But what does that look like?

We Won't Focus on Something Else

To be mentally present, we have to make the decision not to think about a pornographic image or a story line or a past lover. We'll concentrate on how much we love our spouse and on how exciting our spouse is. That will be virtually impossible if we are still filling our minds with porn or erotica. *So you must give that up.* Just like an alcoholic has to say no to alcohol, say no to what is stealing your sexual energy.

For many people, making this change means accountability. Get controls on your computer. Share your account on your e-reader so your spouse can see what you're reading. Get a same-sex accountability partner who you can have coffee with and who will challenge you to remain faithful in every way—and do the same for them.

We'll Give Ourselves Grace

Remaining mentally present is tricky when we have a history with porn. If either of you is shortcutting the arousal cycle by depending on pornographic images, ask God to help you stop, then practice just being present. Think about your body. Think about your spouse. Trace your fingers along your spouse's body. Think specifically about what is feeling good and what you love about your spouse, and mention some of these out loud. Keep your mind focused on the here and now, and you'll find it a much more intimate, and intense, experience.

If you find that mental images interfere, stop what you're doing for a minute, and just talk and kiss again until you find that your mind is back where it should be.

If your spouse is the one trying to break free from porn, extend grace to them. Yes, it can hurt to know that your spouse struggles with fantasy, but giving them a safe place to admit when they're struggling is so much better than humiliating them and making them afraid to tell you when they struggle. If you want honesty and intimacy in the bedroom, you have to give your spouse room to admit when they're having problems—and you have to dedicate yourself to helping them get over them. Remember, focus on the direction you're going, not the place you have come from. Don't get mad at the past; join together to head toward a better sex life for your future.

Great Sex Challenge Day 21

We last talked about porn and erotica after the day 2 challenge, with the optional challenge about dealing with porn. But this is such an important topic that we must revisit it. If you struggle with fantasy or porn and you haven't confessed that to your spouse, take that leap tonight. Reassure your spouse that you want to be mentally faithful and to experience intense passion. Commit to mental fidelity. Revisit that optional challenge and commit to concrete steps to end porn or erotica use. If the porn use is in the past, but flashbacks or fantasies still bother you, confess that and ask your spouse to help you overcome this struggle.

If you're the spouse being confessed to, have grace for your spouse, especially if they are sincere about wanting to change. Remember that many porn and erotica habits predate the marriage, and these fantasies may be something your spouse has been trying to deal with alone for quite some time.

Tonight, if you feel your mind wandering while making love, stop the fantasies by focusing on your spouse. Talk out loud. Think to yourself, "What feels good? What do I want him/her to do now?" Concentrate on your spouse's body and on what your own body is experiencing. And tell your spouse if you need to pause or start over. If your spouse wants to stop and take things slowly, reassure your spouse that this is okay. Dealing with these issues is better than having something stand in the way of real intimacy!

TRY NEW POSITIONS

It may seem strange to be talking about positions in the section on spiritual intimacy, but for the next few days, I want to explore how we decide what's okay to do and how we can spice things up in the bedroom without compromising intimacy.

One of the problems many couples have is that they see sex almost solely in physical terms. Sex is more about pleasure than about closeness.

I think it should be both. And yet when couples discuss their sexual boundaries, they often enter a land mine zone. If we forget that sex is supposed to be intimate and not only orgasmic, we go astray and cheapen sex. And if we make sex about one person's desires, we can take away the mutuality of sex and turn it into an ugly obligation, which also changes the very nature of sex. So I put these few challenges within the spiritual intimacy section to remind us that when we try new things, it should be to increase the fun quotient and to feel closer, not to humiliate anyone or to act selfishly, and certainly not to coerce anybody into something they are uncomfortable with. Coercion has no place in healthy relationships.

With that said, exploring new things, when done right with both people's preferences taken into account, can often lead to more passion. So let's talk today about positions.

I've heard it said that the man-on-top, woman-on-bottom position is called the "missionary position" because missionaries taught that it was the only "proper" position. But that's a myth that makes missionaries sound uptight! Is there a "holy" position? And if we're talking about experiencing spiritual intimacy and not just physical intimacy, are some positions "wrong" and some positions "right"?

I firmly believe that any way two married adults choose to engage in vaginal intercourse is perfectly fine. You're just joining your bodies, and it's not like only the missionary position is ordained by God. In fact, position is never even talked about in the Bible.

The missionary position is often thought to be "holier" because it allows the couple to kiss and look into each other's eyes. But so does the woman-on-top position or the making-love-while-sitting (or even standing) position. So that argument doesn't hold water.

I think the reason the missionary position is thought of as "holy" is because sex is often thought of as shameful (especially for women). Any position that involves a woman being active is often thought of as a little bit wrong (or even a lot wrong). It's somehow unseemly. A man can thrust, because males are supposed to feel sexual pleasure. But for a woman to want to move—well, that may mean she's enjoying herself too much. That's why I think the missionary position developed the reputation of being the "proper" position!

That doesn't mean I'm against it—not at all! For many women it's quite pleasurable. And it is romantic. Nevertheless, it has some drawbacks. It's difficult if there's a big weight discrepancy between the two of you or if she's pregnant. If she's nervous, feeling in control by being on top often relieves some stress. And stimulating the G-spot is usually easier using other positions.

Often a couple will find that one or two positions tend to be their go-tos because she has an easier time reaching climax. Yet trying and using new positions has benefits other than just orgasm. It makes sex more active and less routine. It requires a bit of extra effort, which tells your spouse, *I'm excited about doing this tonight.* It can even increase intimacy because it says to your spouse, *I really want to explore you and know everything I can about how you work.* Trying new positions leads to a new level of vulnerability, which can also increase our feeling of closeness.

One couple I know uses the "Rule of 3"—they can't make love in the same position more than three times in a row. They must switch it up so that it doesn't get boring. If you find it easier to orgasm in one particular position, that's okay. Just use the other positions as foreplay.

So what is a new position? All positions are a variation of four basic ones, which revolve around two factors:

- Who is the main one moving?
- Are they facing each other or not?

Vary those, and there are an infinite number of positions! The first three positions—man-on-top, woman-on-top, side by side—have the couple facing each other and are distinguished by who is doing most of the moving (him, her, or both together, respectively). The last position, rear entry, is distinguished because they're facing in the same direction, with him entering her vagina from behind. Each of these positions has as many variations as the imagination allows, but here are some pointers to get you started.

Man-on-Top

The "missionary position": you lie together, him on top, nose to nose, breast to breast.

Make it feel great: Tilt her hips up. Use a pillow if you want, but the important thing is to engage her muscles to apply pressure to the clitoris, not just to raise her hips.

VARIATIONS

- She puts her legs on his back (or his shoulders, if she can) to allow for deeper penetration.
- She puts her legs between his to allow her more control.
- He kneels or stands while she lies, to give him more leverage to thrust.
- She sits on an object, like a counter or a desk, while he stands.
- And any others you can think of!

*(One warning: Be **very careful** before trying this while he is standing and she is against a wall. Never try anything where her weight could rest on his penis, or you could cause a penile fracture. No matter what variation you try, make sure that she bears her own weight.)*

Woman-on-Top

He lies down in bed, and she climbs on top of him in a sitting position. This position allows her to maneuver more easily to get the best angle, but it also gives him a great view—and easier access to touch different parts of her!

Make it feel great: Let her determine the depth of thrusting, and let her vary the angle until she gets the most contact with her clitoris. For women who are more nervous, or who feel more comfortable being in control, this is often the best position.

VARIATIONS

- She can lie down against him, similar to missionary position but with her on top. The thrusting will then take more energy (and likely burn more calories).
- She sits on him instead of kneeling, with her feet in front of her rather than behind her. This allows for deeper penetration.
- He sits on a chair, and she straddles him.

Side by Side

They lie down, side by side, and one puts their leg over the other. For this one to work well, you both have to move! Getting the right angle can be a little tricky.

Make it feel great: Lean backward to change the angle a bit.

VARIATIONS

- Get in position and roll around until he's on top or she's on top!
- One of you can also lean up, putting weight on your arms, to achieve a different angle.

Rear Entry

She kneels on all fours on the bed. He kneels behind her, facing the same direction. This position is the most difficult to get right because sometimes you have to play around with the angle to achieve penetration. This isn't a position to try early on your honeymoon if you're a virgin on your wedding day. Get comfortable fitting together first. But once you do, some couples swear that this position feels the most pleasurable.

Make it feel great: He can reach around and put a finger or two on her clitoris to increase stimulation. She can also vary the angle of her body so that the penis meets her at different angles. Some women find this is the best way to find the G-spot. And how do you know when you find it? He'll be thrusting, and you'll suddenly feel like you're about to orgasm, even if you hadn't been very aroused yet.

VARIATIONS

- Lie in bed on your sides, facing the same direction, with him behind. This "spooning" position is often the easiest position to use during the latter stages of pregnancy.

- Start with the woman-on-top position, but then have her rotate so she's facing toward his feet. This allows him to touch her breasts easily too.
- She kneels with her head lower against the bed and her hips higher while he stands. This gives him the greatest control (and should only be done slowly, with her setting the pace).

Great Sex Challenge 22

Pick at least three variations, and try all of them tonight! Start with one and then move on to the others. Afterward talk about the following: Would you like to implement something like the "Rule of 3," where you use different positions? Is there a position you like best or find most pleasurable? Share that with your spouse.

DECIDE YOUR SEXUAL BOUNDARIES

In any marriage, one spouse is going to feel more adventurous in the bedroom than the other.

Last week we concentrated primarily on how to create fireworks. Then this week we turned to how to experience spiritual intimacy and oneness when we make love. It's good to have both of those as the context for what we're going to talk about today.

How do you decide what's okay to do and what's not? Let's look at some basic ground rules that can help us.

Our Whole Body Is for Sex

Sex is supposed to be fun. God made our bodies to feel great during sex—and he didn't create sex for only certain body parts to feel good. As we learned in the week on foreplay, the more body parts you involve, the better! When you read Song of Songs, you find tributes to just about every physical attribute. We're supposed to get lost in each other and to enjoy all of each other. That's part of the celebration of being intimate and naked together.

Sex Is More Than Physical

At the same time, sex is more than just a physical connection. It's also a spiritual and emotional connection. One of the reasons, I believe, that married Christians tend to enjoy sex more than those who aren't married is that we know it isn't just about the physical act. When we make love, we also express our commitment to each other and fulfill our hunger for true intimacy.

As we've covered, our culture doesn't understand that because society has divorced sex from relationship and commitment, and so all they have is the physical. That's why our culture has become increasingly pornographic. When the physical is all you have, eventually the physical feels empty. To get the same high, you have to use more and more extreme methods (in the same way that an alcoholic needs more alcohol to get the same buzz). That's going to impact our own ideas of sexuality. If these extreme things—threesomes, sex toys, watching porn together, etc.—are what is portrayed as sexy, then those will entice some of us.

My caution is this: While there is freedom in the marriage bed, and while the whole body is good, if you start seeing sex in terms of riskier and more perverse things, you may lessen its ability to truly bring you and your spouse together intimately. You'll lose the spiritual connection. Be careful to always experience sex first as a way to say I love you and not just as a way to meet selfish fantasies.

There Is Great Freedom

There is great freedom in the marriage bed, and I'd be hesitant to pronounce anything that does not involve a third party—or fantasizing specifically about a third party (like pornography)—as sinful. That being said, just because something isn't sinful doesn't mean it's good to do. As Paul reminds us in 1 Corinthians 6:12, "'I have the right to do anything,' you say—but not everything is beneficial."

While Acts May Not Be Sinful, Selfishness Is

One more caveat, and I'm going to use oral sex as an example. I don't believe oral sex is sinful. Kissing is fine, and the mouth has more germs than most other parts of the body, so if you'll kiss a mouth, I don't think there's a big problem with kissing other parts of the body.

However, I recently received an email from a woman who said her husband demands that they start every encounter this way—and often do this in place of intercourse. He prefers her performing oral sex on him to any shared physical pleasure. That's just pure and simple selfishness.

There is nothing wrong with being "giving" during a particular sexual encounter and concentrating on one of you for a time. But if that becomes the majority of your sex life together, there is a problem. That's not real intimacy; that's being selfish. It needs to stop. In a similar vein, insisting on sexual acts that degrade or humiliate your spouse does not enhance oneness; it detracts from it. You're saying, "I don't value you as a person; I want to use you." That's selfish. Similarly, insisting on an act that can cause physical pain or physical harm is not just selfish; it's coercive and cruel.

Let me say something to those of you who are the more adventurous spouse: it's selfish to demand something that your spouse is truly not comfortable giving. While there's nothing wrong with oral sex, for instance, if a spouse really doesn't want to do it, then you should never, ever push them. Why would you break trust with someone you love? The marriage bed is meant to be an extremely safe place. If you turn it into something unsafe because you insist on something your spouse doesn't want to do, then you're endangering something precious.

Besides, if it isn't really sinful—or even that extreme—you'll likely find that if you spend time being giving and helping your spouse to relax and feel wonderful in bed, then they will be far more willing, and even eager, to try new things.

Finally, one more thing that I want to be absolutely clear about: never, ever force your spouse to do something they don't want to do.

Not only can this be selfish; it may also veer into the illegal. Forcing your spouse to do something they don't want to do constitutes rape. Just because you're married doesn't mean rape can't occur. Additionally, pressuring someone by withholding affection, love, or money if they don't comply can also make your spouse feel they don't have a choice. Criticizing, giving the silent treatment unless they comply, or telling your spouse that you'll be forced to watch pornography if they don't meet your demands has the same effect. Don't ever force your spouse to do something, whether through physical force or emotional or financial manipulation. And if you feel as if your spouse is forcing you, please seek out help through an abuse hotline.

I know that's heavy, but it has to be said!

Dare Yourself

Now, after that big caveat, a word to the spouse who isn't as adventurous. It's okay to say no to some things you really find distasteful. But if they aren't sinful or dangerous, I'd encourage you to ask yourself *why* you think they're distasteful. There may be some ways you can incorporate some of these ideas into your love life in a nonthreatening way, and I'll look at some of them in the next challenge.

Some men enjoy trying various positions and getting creative in the bedroom more often than women do (though there are exceptions). This is logical. Women are far more physically vulnerable in sex. Changing positions can be difficult to get used to. Some positions can make us feel more vulnerable, and some can even be uncomfortable. Once we find a position that works for us with an angle that makes us feel great, we're often less willing to try other ones.

It's okay to say no to some ideas. But then dare yourself to make what you do enjoy absolutely amazing for your spouse! If you're doing that, and you're making love with regular frequency, you'll likely find that trying some of your spouse's other suggestions becomes less of an issue in your marriage.

Great Sex Challenge 23

Today's challenge has three parts!

Part 1: Feel each other's whole bodies. Have one of you start at one foot, and go up one side of your spouse's body, touching and licking or squeezing or whatever you want, all the way to the top of the head, then all the way down the other side. Then switch roles!

Part 2: Once you've done that, have an honest discussion about some of the things you'd like to try, that you're scared of trying, or that you have already done but you really didn't like. Some couples find it easier to talk about this with the lights off so they can't see each other's faces, or while spooning so they're not facing each other.

Part 3: At the end, affirm to each other how much you love and cherish each other—whatever you do in the bedroom. That spiritual connection is always what's most important!

7 Ways to Spice Things Up

For the last two days, we've been talking about stretching the boundaries of what we do during sex—and how we negotiate those boundaries. Today I want to turn this into a more practical, smorgasbord-style challenge and to look at different ways you can become more adventurous in your marriage while remaining comfortable.

Remember the guidelines we set yesterday: no one should ever be pressured to do something they're uncomfortable with or feel is sinful or dangerous. It is never worth jeopardizing the safety of the marriage bed by pushing something on your spouse!

That being said, more often we hesitate to stretch our boundaries because:

1. We're a little scared of something new.
2. We think we may not be able to do it right.
3. We're embarrassed.
4. We're afraid that if we try something new, our spouse will want it all the time.
5. We don't think it's sinful, and we don't think it's wrong. It's just not our cup of tea.

Today I am speaking only to people in one of those five categories. I am not speaking to anyone who is saying no because they have moral reservations, they are completely and utterly grossed out, or they have flashbacks from sexual abuse. If that describes you, it is perfectly fine to say no. But again, make sure you're not saying something is morally wrong just because it isn't the "missionary position." Sometimes we're too quick to label things as morally wrong (though, of course, some things, like porn, definitely are).

Here are some ideas to help you be more adventurous, without violating your sense of decorum.

Give "Love Coupons"

We often hesitate sexually because we ask ourselves, "Do I really want to do this? Is this too wild for me?" We can also be hesitant to do some things we actually want to do because we're shy and feel awkward. We get so caught up in analyzing the scenario that we're not able to make a decision. Emailing your spouse a "coupon" that says "Tonight you own me for an hour" or "Anything you want is yours tonight" can get around that awkwardness.

None of this, however, replaces consent. If you're going to try new things, set up a safe word, like *uncle*, that you can say when you feel like it's too much. Yes, even if you give coupons, you still have autonomy and can say no.

Create His and Hers Nights

Make one evening a month for him, where you cater to his wants. Then one evening a month can be for her, where you do what she wants—like starting with a long back massage and then being very gentle. This way each of you feels as if your needs are met, and you both go out of your way to make the other person's night fun because you know it will be reciprocated!

Write Down Fantasies

Both of you write down twelve sexual fantasies. Don't show your spouse what's on your sheet of paper. Rip or cut up the list, fold up the papers, and put them in a jar. Over the next year, pick one night a month when she'll do a dare and one night when he will. Then, on those nights, draw a piece of paper out of the jar and do what it says. Again, the rules about saying "uncle" still apply; you never *have* to do anything. But if you each have items in the jar, and you know it's a give-and-take, then your spouse can feel like you're going out of your way to meet their needs without your feeling like you have to do it every night.

Play Match-the-Dice

Get two dice of different colors, and write on a sheet of paper what each die means.

First Die—Actions

Choose six actions, like kiss, stroke, lick, rub, flick, suck, and assign them to the six sides of the die.

Second Die—Parts of the Body

Assign the six sides of the second die to six body parts, like mouth, fingers, ears, toes, genitals, breasts.

Take turns throwing the dice, and do whatever combination comes up! You can make the game as adventurous or as tame as you want by varying the actions or body parts. Make sure you give enough time—let's say at least a minute—to each task.

Play Match-an-Activity

As a variation on the Match-the-Dice game, instead of matching an action with a body part, assign a specific activity to each number on the die (you could do six or twelve or somewhere in between, depending on how many activities you want to use). Each of you assign activities to three numbers on the die—things that drive you wild (or if you want to use an eight-sided or twelve-sided die, then you each get more options!). These can be mild, like deep kissing or blowing and teasing and sucking his ear, or more adventurous, like watching her rub lotion on her breasts, performing oral sex, or using a specific sexual position. Then use a timer app on your phone, roll the die, and take turns doing each activity for two minutes. This constant starting-and-stopping delays orgasm for quite a while, so when it finally does happen, it's much more intense.

Sometimes what we want each other to do can stretch our boundaries a bit. So write out your lists, with a few extras, and then read your lists together. You can veto ones you're very uncomfortable with, but try to keep at least one that stretches you. Trying the action for a maximum of two minutes makes it less intimidating while making your spouse feel loved because you're willing to try something new.

Play Pick-a-Position

Here's another idea involving a die and a timer!

Each of you write down your three favorite positions, then assign them to numbers on the die. If you each pick the same position, then you can add variations to it (like sitting or standing, or in a chair, or legs up or legs down). Then roll the die, and do whatever it says for two minutes. Set the timer for two minutes again, and roll the die again.

Incidentally, this often helps men last a little longer because the stimulation is start-and-stop, which can help prolong the experience.

Create a Multisensory Experience

We have five senses: sight, hearing, touch, taste, and smell. Write down each of the senses on a piece of paper and put them in a jar. Alternate nights, and on your night, pick out three pieces of paper and create a sexual experience that uses those three senses.

Often we use only one sense—touch. We make love with the lights off, we don't say much, and we don't really even taste. So figure out a way to engage the other senses! For sight, she can wear something pretty to bed. For taste, use flavored lip balm, or feed her some chocolate! For hearing, tell her your favorite sexual memory you've shared. For smelling, you can put perfume somewhere and ask him to find it. Be creative!

Challenge yourself to come up with ideas for each sense when it's your night so that you're always changing things up a bit.

There you have it! Seven ways to become more adventurous in your sex life while remaining comfortable. If you are regularly taking steps to spice things up and making love with relative frequency, your spouse will feel as if your sex life is exciting, which is what you want—for both of you.

Great Sex Challenge Day 24

Pick one idea and do it! If you're uncomfortable, start with the basic dice game, and take away the options that you're uncomfortable with and replace them with slightly tamer ideas. Sometimes just challenging ourselves to try something—anything—will help us see that sex can be a fun celebration we share with each other.

If you have a lot of fun with this challenge, feel free to make it last several days. Choose one option one night, then try another option the next night. Lather, rinse, repeat! Move on to the next challenge when you're ready.

Heads up: tomorrow's challenge is one that is easier done during the day. So either read the challenge together in the morning, or commit to doing the challenge together the next day.

QUICKIES CAN BE FUN!

There's nothing wrong with a quickie!

We've talked about how to spice things up in bed by trying different positions or stretching our comfort zones. But there's another way to spice things up, and that's a "quickie"—a sexual interlude where the goal is usually to have one of you reach climax as fast as possible.

Now I know I've been arguing that sex should be wonderful for both of you and that it should connect us on a physical, emotional, and spiritual level. How does a quickie fit in with that? Doesn't it sound like the exact opposite?

I don't think so. While I think the sum total of the relationship should be one where you both experience tremendous sexual pleasure and where you both connect on a profound level, not every single encounter needs to be like that. Having an encounter where you're just laughing and it's almost like a game can connect you in a profound way too, because learning how to play with each other is such a key component to feeling close.

So why a quickie? After all, if we women need foreplay to feel good, then quickies aren't going to do much for us, are they? Here are some benefits.

You Laugh

If you've ever run upstairs while the kids are in front of a video, knowing that you have very little time, it's funny. Then you finish, go back downstairs, and pretend like nothing happened. It's like you both share a little secret.

You Add Variety

It's good to do things differently sometimes. It shows both of you that you care about the relationship and that you want to keep it fun. If the quickie is to give her an orgasm through oral sex or manual stimulation, she gets out of the "sex is for him" rut that she may often get in, and he shows that he values "foreplay" acts too!

She Sees How Much He Wants Her

Ladies, do you feel insecure about your bodies? Feel like you're not attractive? A quickie where intercourse-for-him is the main event is often the cure. Most men (hopefully) go to great lengths to make themselves last because they want you to have a good time too. But tell him to go as fast as he can because you have to beat the clock or the video or the baby's nap or whatever it might be, and suddenly you'll see how much he really does love and desire you. It can be a big ego boost—and that ego boost is also an aphrodisiac since a large part of the female libido is feeling desired.

She Boosts Her Libido While Calming His Down

If he often can't last long enough during intercourse for her to get real satisfaction, quickies can help! If you have a quickie early in the day, he satisfies the physical buildup he feels. But she rarely does (some women, of course, do find quickies satisfying, but that's the minority). Instead, she starts her libido charging. Then, the next time you make love, he's more likely to last longer, and she's more likely not to take as long.

You Lower His Stress

Because many men worry about their wives receiving pleasure, they often don't get to relax during an encounter. Quickies let them just focus on the pleasure, which can be very intense.

You Lower Her Stress

Men aren't the only ones nervous about women receiving pleasure. We women often get quite nervous about it too, especially if we're trying to orgasm. Take the pressure off by "giving him a gift." And a quickie can boost her confidence, especially if she feels aroused without expecting to feel much.

So how does a quickie work best?

Grab five minutes—any five minutes. If he's stressed about work today, try a quickie right before he leaves in the morning. Or maybe right when he gets home. Or right before you head out for a date night. Or if she's had a rough day, he can lift up her skirt and go to town!

Have lubricant on hand. Quickies are no fun if you're not lubricated, so keep some lubricant handy!

Just go with it. Don't worry about doing it right. Just laugh through it! You'll feel emotionally closer because you've shared the experience. And you'll both feel desired.

Great Sex Challenge 25

For Her: Sometime in the next week, grab him and take him upstairs! This challenge can be difficult to do right away if you're reading this at night together, so save this challenge until you can do it spontaneously first thing in the morning, during the day, or in the evening when the kids are in bed but before you turn in. Feel free to move on to the next challenge tomorrow night, but try to squeeze a quickie into your schedule soon.

For Him: If your wife orgasms easily through oral sex or manual stimulation, then plan a quickie for her as well! Remember that it's more likely to be fun for her if you don't catch her when she's worried about the children or another responsibility she has. And if orgasm isn't something that's natural for her yet, then keep this challenge in mind for a time in your marriage when this does happen more regularly.

WHY YOU'VE GOT TO INITIATE

What matters in a marriage is not so much the frequency of sex (though that is important) as the enthusiasm and the passion. Your spouse needs to feel like you actually desire and want sex, and not just that you are willing to go through the motions.

Many women (and I'm going to talk about women here because the opposite isn't quite true, since men can't do the deed if they're not interested) complain that when they start "letting" him make love more frequently, he gets even more demanding. So they just give up. They think, "I'll never satisfy him, so why bother?" But the problem may be that you haven't met his basic need to feel desired. In fact, if you just lie there and don't participate much, you reinforce the idea that you don't enjoy sex. That's going to cause him to desperately want to make sure that you do desire him, so he will become *more* urgent about wanting sex. Male commenters on my blog repeatedly tell me that their big desire is not just to have sex. It's to feel as if their wives want them. "Duty sex" leaves them unfulfilled.

Higher-libido wives, too, share this basic need, and this basic desperation. They need to feel desired, and always having to chase your husband can be humiliating.

At this point, though, lower-libido spouses may be just about ready to give up. *It's not enough that I have sex? I actually have to want it? How can I force myself to think of it spontaneously and want it?*

Allow me to give you an idea: Initiate it. Really. *You* be the one to give your spouse a big kiss and say, "Let's go upstairs." *You* start the whole process, rather than waiting to see if your spouse is "going to want to tonight." What's in it for you, you ask? Here are just a few benefits.

You Have More Control over What You Do

We talked earlier about how important angle and foreplay are to women. Ladies, if you initiate, you can take more care that you get the right position and the attention you need. Also, if you're uncomfortable about certain parts of sex (or even uncomfortable about certain parts of your body), then you can steer the moment in a direction that's more comfortable for you.

You Throw Yourself into It More

By initiating, you're automatically more active. You're not just lying there, waiting for your spouse to do something. You're the one touching. You're the one passionately kissing. You're the one undressing. Since you can then steer the action in the direction that's most exciting for you, you're also thinking more positively about what's happening, because you know that what's pleasurable for you is coming up. When you're more active, your brain is also more engaged, and that means your body will follow much more readily!

You Create a Goodwill Circle

When you initiate, you show your spouse that you love and desire him (or her). That makes your spouse feel better about you and about the relationship and makes both of you feel closer to each other.

In a marriage, if one person does all the initiating, that person, whether male or female, will feel as if the other spouse doesn't desire that kind of intimacy. That's a lonely feeling.

If you know you're likely going to make love tonight anyway, why not make the extra effort to be the one to suggest it, or to try to seduce your spouse? When it's a two-way street, you each feel desired, you each feel loved, and you each feel close to each other. When one is always doing the asking, it's humiliating. You feel as if you're constantly begging.

Healthy couples both initiate. So if you're the lower-drive spouse, decide that you'll take the reins more often—starting now.

Great Sex Challenge 26

Without showing your spouse, write down how many times, out of ten, you initiate, how many times you think your spouse initiates, and how many it's mutual. Then compare notes. Do you agree? Does one of you initiate more than the other? Talk to each other about how this makes you feel. Then ask each other, "What would be a good way to initiate? What would be fun for you?" See how many ideas you can each come up with! And now, for the lower-desire spouse, pick one and do it!

DAYS 27–31

Keep the Momentum Going!

MAKE SEX A PRIORITY

We've looked at how to have more fun together, how to see sex in a more positive light, how to make sex feel amazing, and how to feel truly intimate. I hope that by this time in the challenge you've experienced some breakthroughs!

However, if you want to keep the momentum going, and keep those breakthroughs coming, then you need to set up a system so that once this 31-day challenge is over, and you don't have something prompting you to work on your sex life regularly, your intimacy remains a priority. These last few challenges will focus on how to keep these changes alive in your marriage.

When I did surveys for *The Good Girl's Guide to Great Sex*, I found that over 40 percent of women reported having sex less than once a week. Drilling down into the numbers, it turned out that the higher-libido spouse (whether it was the wife or the husband) wasn't overly pleased with this.

Frequency is always a tricky question when it comes to sex because every marriage has some libido differences. So how often is enough? If I were forced to pick a number, I would say at least twice a week. But for some couples, especially when they're younger, more would probably be healthier. And the happiest couples I found were those who were making love three to four times a week. Connecting that often has repercussions on how you feel about each other.

Maybe we should stop asking, "What's the minimum I can get away with?" and start asking, "How can I make sex a better part of both of our lives?" After all, if God made sex to be awesome, why would we want to miss out on that?

Often the reason we miss out isn't because we don't want sex but simply because other things get in the way. So today I'd like to use some principles from economics to help us find a solution to this frequency problem. Perhaps it's because I ended up taking Economics 101 three times over my life—in high school, in undergraduate courses, and in postgraduate courses—but I had demand and supply drilled into me so much that I often think in those terms. I think we can apply these concepts to how frequently sex happens too! Let's try.

Basic economics tells us that the "price" of something is where the demand for it intersects with the supply of it. The demand for something tends to increase when the price drops, while the supply tends to decrease when the price drops.

But what determines how much of a product will be supplied at each point? The cost of the inputs. So if you were making ice cream, for instance, and the price of milk dropped, then the supply line would shift, and the price of ice cream would decrease.

In the following graph that will make anyone who ever took Economics 101 cringe, you can see that the demand and supply meet at eleven times per month. But what happens when an input cost drops? Suddenly more will be supplied at each price point, and bingo! You now have sex thirteen times a month.

That may sound complicated, but I hope you get the picture: when inputs are more expensive, you're going to get less of something because people won't buy as much at the higher price. That's why if the government wants you to buy less of something (like tobacco), they tax it, but if they want you to buy more of something (like charity), they give you a tax deduction.

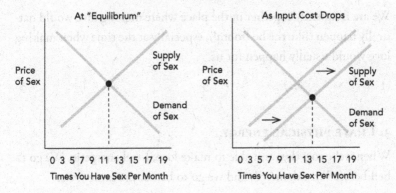

An Economic Way of Looking at Sex

What does this mean for sex?

It means that if the cost of sex gets too high, you'll have less sex.

If we want to have great sex in marriage, we've got to keep the cost of inputs down!

Great Sex Challenge 27

Today's challenge is going to be a little different. I'm going to list a number of "inputs" into sex, and then both of you separately rate the cost of those inputs, with 1 being super cheap (as in *I agree with the statement, and this factor isn't keeping us from making love more frequently*"), and 5 being very expensive (as in "*The statement is not true for me, and this is really deterring sex*").

I. WE HAVE A PLACE TO MAKE LOVE.

Our bedroom is clutter-free and kid-free. When we go into the bedroom, we feel peaceful and calm. The bed is free of other stuff, and the bed itself is inviting.

| 1 | 2 | 3 | 4 | 5 |

2. WE HAVE TIME TO MAKE LOVE.

We are frequently together in the place where making love would naturally happen (like the bedroom!), especially at the time when making love would usually happen for us.

1	2	3	4	5

3. I HAVE PHYSICAL ENERGY.

When we're together and able to make love, I feel energetic. We go to bed before I'm exhausted, and we go to bed at the same time.

1	2	3	4	5

4. I FEEL PHYSICALLY WELL.

I feel physically able to make love without impediment. I'm not burdened by chronic pain, migraines, nausea, or other ailments.

1	2	3	4	5

5. I FEEL EMOTIONALLY REPLENISHED.

When evening comes, I feel replenished. I have time to get my needs for solitude and reflection and meaning met during the day so that we can be together at night.

1	2	3	4	5

6. I FEEL MENTALLY CALM.

I tend to feel peaceful and calm. I'm able to shut off the demands of work, running the household, or family troubles so that we can be together.

1	2	3	4	5

7. I FEEL GOOD ABOUT MY BODY.

I'm comfortable in my own skin. Even though I don't think my body is perfect, I do enjoy my body, and I don't mind showing it to my spouse.

1	2	3	4	5

8. I FEEL EMOTIONALLY CLOSE.

I feel close to my spouse. I feel as if we share life together, that we're partners, and that we do a lot of fun things together. I truly feel as if we're best friends.

1	2	3	4	5

9. I TRUST MY SPOUSE.

I can trust that my spouse thinks of me as their only object of desire. I can trust my spouse not to use pornography and not to be thinking about other people.

1	2	3	4	5

10. I ENJOY MY SPOUSE'S SCENT.

I enjoy how my spouse smells. I feel as if my spouse has good hygiene.

1	2	3	4	5

11. SEX CAN BE STRESS-FREE.

The repercussions of sex don't scare me. I'm confident in our contraception methods, and I'm not scared of either getting pregnant or not getting pregnant.

1	2	3	4	5

12. SEX ISN'T MESSY.

I'm not worried about the mess of sex. When we have sex, I can easily drift off to sleep afterward with a minimum of fuss (after going to the bathroom, for instance). I don't feel the need to change sheets or take a shower.

1	2	3	4	5

13. I LOOK FORWARD TO A GOOD TIME.

When I know we're going to have sex, I have confidence that I'm going to orgasm and feel good.

1	2	3	4	5

14. I'M NOT WORRIED ABOUT PAIN OR THINGS GOING WRONG.

When we make love, I'm not worried that I'll feel pain, and I'm not worried that one of us won't be able to perform sexually.

1	2	3	4	5

Once you've rated these statements separately, pull out your answers and compare them. Take a look at the two answers she rated costliest, and the two that he did (or, if you rated more than two as very costly, decide your top two). Make a plan to "reduce" the cost of this input. Maybe it means going back and redoing some of the exercises. Maybe it means going to bed at the same time or finding ways to destress during the day. Maybe it means seeing a doctor or a physiotherapist.

Once you've made a plan, talk about how you can prioritize sex more. Over the next few days, we'll look in greater detail at how to deal with some of the most common roadblocks to having sex more frequently. However, you can start those conversations tonight! Discuss what frequency is reasonable given your work schedules, kids, and stage of life, and then decide what practical steps you can take to make that easier to achieve—even if you have to schedule sex!

Is Scheduling Sex for You?

THE PROS OF SCHEDULING SEX

You Make Sex a Priority

Let's face it: often we don't end up making love because it's the last thing on our to-do list. *If* the dishes are done and *if* the kids go to bed at a decent time and *if* my emails are all answered and *if* I feel 100 percent and *if* I'm not ticked at my spouse and *if* I don't have to be up early, then when I hit the pillow at eleven, I may consider having sex.

There's a lot working against sex!

So sex is often put on the back burner, even though it is important for helping a marriage to stay intimate and fun and helps each of us feel invigorated about life and our relationship.

If you schedule it and decide that every Wednesday and every Saturday you'll have sex, then you know you'll connect. And you know you'll feel intimate again. In most marriages sex isn't frequent enough; here's one way to overcome that!

It Reminds You to Get Your Head in the Game

For women, so much of our sex drive is in our heads. When our heads are in the game, our bodies often follow. But it's hard to get your head in the game if you're just going about your normal routine with kids or your job or the housework. But if you know you're going to have some fun tonight, you can think more positively about it. You can flirt with your husband more, send secret texts, or even just remind yourself of the last great time you connected.

For all lower-libido spouses, scheduling sex ends the tension of the "Do I want to tonight?" question that often tortures us. You know you're going to tonight, so you don't have to figure out if you're in the mood. You just decide to think of sex positively and get ready to jump in.

You Are More Likely to Take Care of Yourself

If you get in the habit of making love a few times a week, it will become evident that you need to get enough sleep! You're more likely to start treating your body better, and sleeping more, because you want to enjoy what's in store. Women may even shave their legs more frequently or spritz on some perfume, and both of you may shower more often and pick out the pajamas without holes in them.

THE CONS OF SCHEDULING SEX
Obligation Sex Isn't Sexy

One of the reasons we do the "Do I want to tonight?" routine is because when we don't feel like it, sex can seem like an imposition. If you agree to schedule sex, and then the night comes around and you really don't feel like it, you can end up resenting sex, and your spouse, even more.

Scheduling sex, then, works only if you're willing to say positive things to yourself about sex. When you schedule sex, you don't just commit to having sex; you commit to having a good attitude about it and being enthusiastic about it. If you schedule sex so that "at least I'll get bugged only on Wednesdays and Saturdays and not all the other days too," it likely won't work well for you, and you're not being fair to your spouse or yourself. Your issue is bigger than just how often you have sex.

Scheduling sex does not eliminate the right of a spouse to say, "Not tonight." If you're feeling ill, if you've got the blues, or if you're overwhelmed by work, sometimes you may have to give a rain check. If scheduling sex makes one of you feel as if your consent doesn't matter (and thus you don't matter), it can make sex feel even worse.

Spontaneity Can Suffer

One of the wonderful things about making love with my husband is that sometimes we're not planning on it. We fall into bed, and we're both tired, and we just hug for a bit and talk. And in the process, something just happens.

If you start scheduling sex, you may limit those moments. It's also important to feel as if your spouse wants you, not just wants to placate you. If you eliminate those times when you turn to each other *just because*, your spouse can feel as if it's not something you want to do; it's just something you feel you have to do.

LET'S PUT IT ALL TOGETHER

For many lower-libido spouses who find it difficult to get motivated for sex, scheduling sex can be a great idea. And here's the great thing: once you make love with relative frequency, you yearn for it. You start to enjoy it. And then it may become more frequent all on its own! You will see the difference that connecting regularly can make in your relationship.

Let me leave you with a few warnings.

Think of the Schedule as the Minimum, Not the Maximum

If you decide to schedule sex on Wednesday and Saturday and you feel a little frisky on a Monday, then do something on Monday! Don't "turn off" those feelings because they weren't scheduled. Feel free to explore them. Scheduling sex should not eliminate spontaneity; it should just make sure you connect regularly, at a minimum.

Decide to Jump In Wholeheartedly

If you decide to schedule sex, pledge that you will put everything into it. Make those nights the best you can. Plan fun things! Flirt. You put effort into other parts of your life; put it in here too.

If you put effort into planning fun activities, then scheduling sex might give your marriage the jump start it needs! But making a schedule can never make up for a lack of enthusiasm or for feeling "at least I'm off the hook now." Jump in with the right attitude, and see the long-lasting benefit to your sex life—and your entire relationship!

ADULTS NEED BEDTIMES TOO!

In most homes today, after dinner is over, various family members separate to their own screens—either the computer or the TV or the video game system. She may be on her iPad, and he's playing games. Eventually somebody gets tired and heads to bed, but the other person doesn't join them for several hours.

And we wonder why we feel disconnected!

How are you going to keep a marriage alive if you scatter at night? How can you nurture your marriage if you never have downtime just to talk? Sure, it's going to be harder to connect sexually if you're not in bed at the same time. But it's harder to connect at all.

As you've worked through these challenges, you've hopefully tried new things, had fun, and had some great conversations. You feel closer and more intimate. But it's going to be difficult to keep that momentum going if you lapse into old patterns of not being together at night.

Many women tell me, "I go to bed at eleven, and he follows around one or two. And then he wakes me up because he wants sex." That's difficult, and extremely inconsiderate.

Before the advent of electricity and the internet, everyone had a bedtime—children *and* their parents. If you needed eight and a half hours of sleep, and you had to get up at six thirty, then you went to bed at ten—and often much earlier, once the sun had set and the candle was done. It was quite simple, and quite civilized.

Let's Get Back to Adult Bedtimes!

I know consistent adult bedtimes aren't possible for everyone when shift work is involved. I know that's a difficult lifestyle, and my husband and I have lived it our whole married life. But many people are home together at night, and they *still* don't go to bed together.

When parents have a hard time getting a child to go to sleep at night, what do experts suggest? Setting up a routine so that the child knows what's coming and has that transition time between daytime and nighttime so they are able to wind down. Maybe the routine looks like this:

- Snack
- Bath
- Story
- Song
- Prayers
- Kiss good night

If we want to improve sex, setting up an adult bedtime ritual can be one of the best things to do because it gets us to bed on time, together. Maybe it looks like this:

- Snack (or cup of tea together)
- Bath or shower together
- Read a chapter of a book or an article or a psalm together out loud
- Snuggle
- Pray
- Make love
- Sleep

Each step leads to the next. That's what makes it a routine—one thing follows another, which follows another, which makes you ready for bed.

Right now the only thing bringing some people to bed is that they fall asleep on the couch, then eventually wake up and move.

Not good.

So tonight, for your challenge, let's figure out a new adult bedtime routine.

Great Sex Challenge 28

First, figure out what time you should go to sleep! Ask yourselves what time you need to get up in the morning. Count backward at least seven and a half or eight hours—that's the time you should go to sleep. Count backward another forty-five minutes—that's the time you should start your bedtime routine.

Now plan your bedtime routine. Talk about these issues: Are screens allowed before bed? If not, what time should you turn them off? What short activities do you each like doing at night that can help you relax? Here are some ideas:

- Drink a hot beverage.
- Read a chapter from a book.
- Take a bath or shower.
- Give each other a massage.
- Plan out your day for tomorrow.
- Talk over your day for tomorrow.
- Read Scripture or some other meditation.
- Pray.

Talk about which ones you'd like to include in a bedtime routine. What order will you do them in?

Decide on a bedtime routine—and try it tonight!

Keep Your Bedroom Inviting

When our children were babies, we lived in a tiny two-bedroom apartment. Our computer was in our bedroom. Our duvet was threadbare and rather ugly. In fact, everything in that room was old and rather ugly.

One winter, after a particularly grueling year during which we were grieving the loss of our little boy, we decided to head south for a vacation to recoup. When we arrived home and walked through the door, we saw that my mother and a friend had redone our bedroom with new bedding, plump new pillows, and a new lamp.

Unfortunately, they couldn't move the computer and all the excess items out of our room, but even the small effort they made created such a transformation. When I walked into our bedroom, I wasn't depressed anymore!

If you're going to keep the changes in your sex life moving forward, you need to have a fun place to connect, and that means having an inviting bedroom. If your dresser is covered with old Visa receipts, if craft boxes are stacked up in a corner, if your bedding is threadbare and ugly and your pillows are lumpy, then climbing into bed isn't fun. And if you figure that your bed is the best place to fold laundry—it's so big, and just the right height!—but then that laundry never gets put away, and every night you sweep it onto the floor again, then jumping into bed isn't going to be stress-free.

If you're scared to step into your bedroom because it's a mess, or if it's just so ugly that you sigh when you walk in, then it's time to change.

But mess and laundry aren't the only things that can make our bedrooms unromantic. What about computers and televisions? Bring a screen into the bedroom, and you're likely to stare at it rather than your spouse. Instead of talking and snuggling, you'll catch the end of *Law & Order*. That's hardly conducive to romance. Work isn't all that romantic either. Flipping through files in bed doesn't help you in the relationship department.

So try to banish screens, mess, and work from your bedroom, and keep it an inviting oasis, away from the rest of the world. Let it be a haven where you can escape, just the two of you.

Great Sex Challenge 29

Look around at your bedroom. Is it inviting? Why or why not? Do you have a TV in your room? Do you often bring computers or phones in? What about work? Discuss with each other how that makes you both feel and what you would each like your bedroom to feel like.

Now, how can you bring peace and fun to your bedroom? Do you need new bedding? New rules about what is allowed in your bedroom?

Once you've decided what you'd like to do, make a date to do it. If your bedroom needs to be cleaned up, set the date by which that will be done. If you need to buy new bedding or new pillows, decide when you're going to do that, and start shopping online right now, or put it on the calendar if you're going to go in person. Spending money on your bedroom is not a selfish extravagance; the best thing you can do for your family is to build a strong marriage. Prioritize that, and everything else falls into place.

SEX AFTER PARENTHOOD

Sex is obviously the start of parenthood, but for many couples, parenthood is often the end of sex. How can you keep your sex life fresh when kids are hanging off you, you're exhausted, and you need some time to yourself? For the last twenty-nine days you've been concentrating on sex and making it a priority. But for these new habits to "stick," you have to change your patterns so that the roadblocks to a healthy sex life are minimized. And for those of us with kids at home, parenting can be one of the biggest roadblocks.

Today's challenge is designed for those with children of any age at home. If you don't have kids at home, you can skip ahead. But if your parenting days are still ahead of you, read on so that you can talk about and plan for how you would like to handle some of these challenges.

Prioritize Marriage

When I speak at women's conferences, I often ask the women, "Are you a better wife or a better mom?" Around 80 percent of the room believe they are better moms. It makes sense. These little beings need us so much, and we love them so much, that children quickly snatch the vast majority of our energy. Our husbands get the leftovers. Men too can pour so much into their kids that there's little left for their wives.

Once you have children, though, your marriage is even more important, not less. Other people are counting on you two being rock-solid together. Your marriage is the foundation for their little lives. You owe it to each other and to your children to put your marriage before the kids.[7]

Keep the Bedroom Safe

If you're going to build a great marriage, you need a safe place in the house where you can be alone, just the two of you.

When my youngest daughter was six, my husband and I were once enjoying a rather good time in bed when we heard that familiar pitter-patter down the hall. We froze, pulled up the sheets, and were grateful when she jiggled the doorknob and realized it was locked. "It's okay!" she yelled, and we heard her go back down the hall. Relieved, we resumed, until about three minutes later the door burst open and the flurry of sheets began again. It turns out that six is old enough to know how to pick a lock but not old enough to know that you don't want to pick that lock.

Keep a good lock on your bedroom door! You can always unlock it after romance is over, but make sure kids can't barge in at inopportune times.

The problems don't end when the children get older. Life with teenagers is often even more trying because teens tend to stay up much later than you do. *And they know what's going on.* One friend shared her story with me. She and her husband had enjoyed a good time, and when it was over, they lay there talking. But their teen daughter's music was so loud that they couldn't hear each other. He got out of bed, opened the door, and yelled, "Jen, how many times do I have to tell you to turn that music down?" She yelled back, "Dad, it's this loud for a reason! *Ick!*"

You can encourage your teens to take part-time jobs so they're out of the house more often. You can encourage them to be in their rooms by a certain time so that everyone can have privacy. You can encourage them all to go to youth group or some other activity that gives you the house to yourselves.

But let's face it. No matter how hard you try to get some privacy, you can't restrict your sex life to only when the teens are out, or your sex life may rapidly become nonexistent. So how about a change of perspective? As much as we may be embarrassed by our kids' knowing what we're doing, a healthy sex life models a healthy relationship. And it gives them a sense of stability.

Don't stop your sex life because you're embarrassed by what the kids may hear. Obviously you don't want to advertise it, but if they figure it out, it isn't the end of the world. Great parents gross out their kids, because they show kids that marriage is not the place that sex goes to die. Married people can love each other and still be passionate for each other.

Yes, learn to be quiet. Turn on the radio to muffle the noise if you need to. But most of all, remember that your marriage comes first, and children will not be scarred by learning that their parents are still hot for each other.

Keep the Bedroom Kid-Free

If you have smaller children, I'd also recommend keeping the bedroom kid-free. When babies are first born, pediatricians recommend the babies sleep in a bassinet or a crib beside your bed. But as they grow, I believe it's best to move children into their own bedrooms. The current guidelines state that this can be done by six months of age.[8] Children can usually learn to sleep through the night at that age, and learning to self-soothe is an important skill that gives them security.

I know not all parents agree on this, and many families swear by the "cosleeping" arrangement where babies and toddlers pile in bed with the parents. If that's what you both agree is best, that is your prerogative.

However, I would like to offer a few warnings. First, quite often one spouse is committed to this arrangement while the other is not. That's not fair. If one spouse really wants the bedroom for the couple, that desire matters.

The second caveat is that it's difficult to have an active, healthy sex life when children are in the bed. Some moms have said to me, "Sheila, you don't need to have sex in the bedroom! We just make a point of having great sex elsewhere in the house!" That's wonderful. But here's the thing: often couples start making love when they didn't plan on it beforehand because they're lying in bed just talking, and things happen. If you have kids in the bed, that easy, low-key spontaneity is gone. Anytime you put up a barrier to sex, you make it less likely to occur. As we talked about earlier, you've increased the price of the "inputs" of sex.

This doesn't mean you *can't* have a great sex life if your kids sleep with you. It simply means you will never have as good a sex life as you could have if your kids were in their own rooms. Please, think carefully about your marriage before you decide to let the children sleep with you with no end in sight. And if you're at the point where you'd like to get them out of your bed but don't know how, some quick Google searches will give you lots of ideas!

Set Up "Couple Time" Evenings—or Mornings

Carving out time to be together as a couple is vital. Setting a regular time for this in your schedule makes it easier to ensure that it happens. When the kids know to expect "couple time," it's not a big deal.

So set up a once-a-week "couple evening," where the children eat an early dinner and then play in their rooms so you can have a more relaxed dinner, just the two of you. Or set up "couple mornings" on Saturdays, when the kids can watch TV for a few hours so that you can stay with each other. Find times that are yours, then set those aside so the kids know what to expect.

Great Sex Challenge 30

Talk honestly with each other about how much the kids are hampering your sex life. Commit together that your marriage comes first, and figure out ways to find some alone time, no matter what the ages of your kids. Ask each other: Do you think I put too much emphasis on the kids and not enough on you? Listen humbly to the answer. Then brainstorm together: How can we carve out couple time? How can we make our bedroom a safe place for us? Identify some concrete steps you can take to keep your couple time sacred and safe.

CELEBRATE

You're at the last day of our 31-day challenge! I hope you've found this month helpful in opening the lines of communication, discovering new things about your spouse (and yourself), and experiencing new fireworks.

In this, our last day, I want both of you to celebrate your relationship and how far you've traveled together. And I invite both of you to look forward, not backward. That mind-set is key if the growth and success you've had so far are to continue.

Imagine this scenario: A wife realizes that over most of their marriage, she hasn't been generous sexually with her husband. She wants things to be different. At the same time, he's been withholding affection because he doesn't feel loved. They both confess this to each other and resolve to go forward together. They're excited about it!

For a few nights, things go wonderfully. But then one night she's extra tired and has a headache. She wants to just go to sleep. He thinks, "Oh, great, here we go again. She said she wanted to change, but she won't. It will never last." And he gets angry. She knows he's angry, and she thinks, "He doesn't care what I've done all week. Sex really is all he thinks about!" They're back to old patterns.

Don't let that be your story! If your spouse has said they want to change, then from this time forward, commit to seeing your spouse

197

through the lens of their new commitment, not the lens of your old experience. If she said she wants to change, and she is changing, then missing a few nights of sex when she has headaches shouldn't be a big deal. But if you're obsessing on the past, it will be.

Perhaps you've always doubted whether your wife really wants you. Perhaps you've always doubted whether your husband truly loves you. Perhaps you wonder whether he's still thinking about the porn and not about you. You have to put these thoughts behind you. If your spouse says they want a new start, and they've taken concrete steps to demonstrate that, believe it! You've hit a reset button on your intimate life and your marriage this month—keep walking forward.

Walking forward is easier to do if you actually change your patterns. Remember way back at the beginning of the 31 days when I suggested learning how to reawaken your body and rediscover each other? That's a wonderful exercise to repeat regularly. It helps you discover new things about each other, but it also prevents you from doing the "typical"—either rushing through sex or touching each other in ways that perhaps you thought were pleasurable but really aren't. Reacquainting yourselves with each other's bodies as if you're doing so for the first time helps you to see your new sex life as separate from the old patterns you followed before this challenge.

And then continue to try new things! If you have tended to make love in a certain way, try something else. Use a different position, a different room, even a different time of day. Change things up occasionally to avoid slipping into old patterns, unhealthy mind-sets about sex, or negative thoughts toward your spouse. When there has been hurt or distrust, it's difficult to put that behind you. Change says to each other: This is a new beginning. We're walking forward in a different way now, with a different outlook.

Hopefully you've learned something and had some great experiences this month. Perhaps you've talked together about important factors in the ongoing health of your marriage. Carry those forward with you. Tonight, in your challenge, you'll celebrate where you've come from, what you've enjoyed, and how you plan to keep moving forward.

Great Sex Challenge 31

First, the practical side of the challenge. What are two or three simple ideas you can put in place to make sure you don't lose the momentum you've built? Maybe they're habits like getting the TV out of the bedroom or going for a walk after dinner. Or perhaps you adopt the "Rule of 3," where you change sexual positions at least every fourth time. Write down your ideas, and share them with each other.

Now the romantic side. Write a letter to your spouse, in detail, covering these four areas:

- Here's what I love about sex with you.
- Here's what I found most sexy that we did this month.
- Here's when I felt closest to you this month.
- Here's what I'm looking forward to in our sex life.

Share your letters with each other. Writing things down means you can save the letters and look at them again later. If you're not a writing person, talk through the questions. But remember: extra effort always pays off!

My Last Word

I'm so glad you embarked on this journey together. My desire is to see marriages thrive so that families and communities can thrive too. And sex is at the center of all of that. As we learn to experience real intimacy and passion, it's going to have amazing ripple effects in other areas of our lives. I pray that this has been a positive experience in your marriage, and I pray that your marriage will only grow stronger from here!

How to Find a Counselor If You Need More Help

Because sex is highly personal and vulnerable, when we have relationship issues or past trauma, we may need professional help to get to a healthy place. I always recommend that couples who are struggling find someone specially trained to talk to, because I hate seeing couples stuck.

However, bad counseling can often be worse than no counseling at all, so if you seek counseling, here are four tips to find a counselor who will be able to help you.

Check Their Credentials

Ideally, look for a licensed counselor who is equipped to deal with marriage and sexual problems. Licensed counselors have specific training in evidence-based therapies, understand the nature and reality of trauma and mental illness, and are usually equipped to deal with issues of abuse. Licensed marriage and family therapists, licensed social workers, licensed clinical psychologists, and psychiatrists all have ethical and professional guidelines they must adhere to, including abiding by clients' privacy, or they risk losing their accreditation. In most cities you can find Christians who have these credentials, and increasingly, many licensed Christian counselors also counsel via Skype.

However, many people call themselves counselors without having licenses, especially those employed by a church. My rule of thumb is this: don't go to a counselor who has credentials that the secular world would not consider valid. Many times in the church we allow for shortcuts because we want to support people pursuing their ministry, even if the ministry includes their being responsible for someone else's health and well-being. Yet you wouldn't go to a doctor or a nurse who has less training simply because they are Christian. We need to have the same standards for our counselors and mental health professionals in the church because they too deal with sensitive, important issues that require a great deal of training and expertise to handle responsibly.

This does not rule out counselors trained by Christian universities, by the way. Many Christian universities have counseling programs that are fully accredited by schools of psychotherapy in the US and Canada. Ask where your counselor trained and what licenses they have, and don't be afraid to google them to check their qualifications.

Make Sure Confidentiality Is Ensured

Licensed counselors, psychologists, and psychiatrists must abide by confidentiality, or they will lose their licenses. They can break confidentiality only if they fear their client is at risk of harming themselves or others, or if a crime is disclosed that they must report to the police.

In many church situations using unlicensed counselors, though, clients are required to sign a consent form that allows the counselor to break confidentiality and inform the pastors or elders if they have any concerns or if there are areas of "persistent sin" (which don't tend to be defined). Given the sensitive nature of what you may discuss with the counselor, it is best to avoid these situations.

Choose Someone Specially Trained in Your Area of Need

Counseling for abuse requires specialized training in specific evidence-based therapies—or treatments that have been studied scientifically and shown to have positive outcomes. But not all counselors have such training. If you are seeking a counselor specifically to treat post-traumatic stress disorder from abuse, ask if they have specific training in therapies with a proven track record, and ask which ones.

Not all counselors are trained in handling abuse in marriage either. If you fear you are in an abusive marriage, ask for their training in abuse, as well as how they define emotional abuse. Unfortunately, many church counseling programs have not handled abuse appropriately in the past, or have downplayed the reality of emotional abuse. If this is your story, ask good questions before you start. Effective, safe counselors know that couples therapy should not be pursued when addressing abusive marriages, but instead only individual therapy is appropriate, since couples counseling often enables the abuser to retraumatize their spouse. Abuse is not a marriage issue but a character issue, and it should be treated as such.

Feel Free to Leave If You Don't Think the Counselor Is a Good Fit

Finally, a counseling relationship is not a commitment. You are seeking counseling to improve your marriage and your mental and emotional health. If you feel as if a counselor is not helping you, or is actively making your situation worse, feel free to find someone who is a better fit for you.

NOTES

1. Sheila's blog: https://tolovehonorandvacuum.com.

2. For a great resource on this, see Bruxy Cavey, *Reunion: The Good News of Jesus for Seekers, Saints and Sinners* (Harrisonburg, VA: Herald, 2017).

3. Pamela Rogers and Ana Gotter, "The Health Benefits of Sex," Healthline, July 29, 2016, https://www.healthline.com/health /healthy-sex-health-benefits.

4. Eliana V. Carraca et al., "Body Image Change and Improved Eating Self-Regulation in a Weight Management Intervention for Women," *International Journal of Behavioral Nutrition and Physical Activity* 8 (July 2011): 75.

5. David Schultz, "Divorce Rates Double When People Start Watching Porn," *Science*, August 26, 2016, https://www.sciencemag.org/news /2016/08/divorce-rates-double-when-people-start-watching-porn.

6. Michael Castleman, "Desire in Women: Does It Lead to Sex? Or Result from It?" *Psychology Today*, July 15, 2009, https:// www.psychologytoday.com/us/blog/all-about-sex/200907/desire -in-women-does-it-lead-sex-or-result-it.

7. This statement that the marriage comes before the kids is true for most marriages that are healthy. Kids' safety, however, is always paramount. Kids are also harmed by witnessing their mother being abused. This book is not intended to fix an abusive marriage, and for those in that situation, please seek out help.

8. "American Academy of Pediatrics Announces New Safe Sleep Recommendations to Protect against SIDS, Sleep-Related Infant Deaths," American Academy of Pediatrics, October 24, 2016, https://www.aap.org/en-us/about-the-aap/aap-press-room/Pages /American-Academy-of-Pediatrics-Announces-New-Safe-Sleep -Recommendations-to-Protect-Against-SIDS.aspx.

The Good Girl's Guide to Great Sex

(And You Thought Bad Girls Have All the Fun)

Sheila Wray Gregoire

Do bad girls really have more fun? Surveys say no. The women who are most likely to enjoy sex are married and religious. In other words, they're good girls! But good girls know that making sex great isn't about acting trashy. It's about recognizing what God really designed sex for and then learning how to reap all these benefits and joyfully enjoy your husband. Frank and contemporary, *The Good Girl's Guide to Great Sex* will give newly engaged women and new brides—and some veteran wives—a Christian resource to answer their most intimate, and embarrassing, questions. In a conversational style, with lots of humorous anecdotes, the book will show that sex isn't just physical: it's also an emotional and spiritual experience. And we'll learn why commitment in a Christian marriage is the perfect recipe for a sex life that is out of this world!

Available in stores and online!

Bring a life-giving marriage experience to your church or group!

Sheila's signature Girl Talk will leave women laughing, crying, and saying, "I can't believe she just said that!" It's a down-to-earth, informative presentation of everything God made sex to be, how it can go haywire, and how you can regain real intimacy in your marriage.

Keith and Sheila's I Choose You, an interactive marriage event, can be held over a weekend or a Saturday. Projects will help couples grasp concepts immediately—and start seeing real change. No more marriage pat answers! Just real-life, biblical solutions for the messiness of life.

For booking information, email sheila@sheilawraygregoire.com.

Sheila talks about sex every day. Connect with her:

ToLoveHonorandVacuum.com

Instagram.com/sheilagregoire

Twitter.com/sheilagregoire

Facebook.com/sheila.gregoire.books

Printed in the USA
CPSIA information can be obtained
at www.ICGtesting.com
JSHW031521140724
66401JS00011B/100

9 780310 358343